Arizona Nuggets

Arizona Centennial Edition

by

Dean Smith

Foreword by

Marshall Trimble

Official Arizona State Historian

Published by
Historic Arizona Press
Attn: Kiwanis Club of Friendship Village
2645 E. Southern Avenue
Tempe, AZ 85282

Library of Congress Control Number: 2009904608

ISBN: 1-4392-4067-1

Arizona Nuggets - Third Edition – February 2012

Cover design by Jennifer Hanson

Table of Contents

Foreword

Dean Smith is one of the most prolific writers in Arizona. He just keeps cranking out one book after another, writing stories about everything from sports figures to ranchers to politicians. If books were babies, Planned Parenthood would be up in arms.

This time he's compiled a book of some ninety-two short stories about Arizona and Arizonans, including lesser known but fascinating people like Elliott Roosevelt, Grady Gammage, and Mrs. Archer Linde. Dean's vignettes often bring out little serendipitous nuggets that cause the reader to exclaim, "I didn't know that!"

Writers love that response.

For example, did you know that FDR's playboy son Elliott had strong Arizona connections? For that matter, did you know he was a playboy?

Or did you know that Grady Gammage had a dream of a magnificent auditorium on the site where a village of Army surplus houses for returning World War II veterans was located? There was also a large field on the site where just three years earlier I had played on the ASU intramural softball championship team.

During the 1950s the main venue for concerts in the Valley was the little auditorium at Phoenix Union High School. Mrs. Archer Linde booked national acts there and had a dream that one day Phoenix would be a great cultural center in the Southwest. Even though she didn't live long enough to see that dream come to fruition it eventually did happen.

That's what so great about Dean's book. It's filled with interesting stories about people who were often left out of the mainstream history books.

"My aim," he says, "is to acquaint newcomers to Arizona – and longer residents, too – who come from all over the country, with a bit of Arizona history."

His "aim" is right on target. His entertaining, easy-to-read stories reflect the wide variety of people who have made a difference in the history of Arizona.

Dean began writing these stories a few years ago to sell in a local gift shop to raise money for charity. Recently Tempe Kiwanis clubs encouraged him to enlarge on his original collection and to publish this book. Profits from sales of this edition will go to Kiwanis clubs to support children's and community programs. They also plan to give copies to schools. Dean will donate his royalties to this good cause.

Dean Smith has been an Arizonan for more than seven decades. Mount Baldy still had hair when he arrived. He has written more than a dozen books on Arizona history, including biographies of two of the state's most illustrious families, the Goldwaters and the Babbitts. He has been a frequent contributor to *Arizona Highways* magazine and edited books for the magazine's book division and for the University of Arizona Press.

Dean grew up in Glendale and has been an eyewitness to the greatest transitional period in Arizona history. During his varied career he has been a sports writer and editor, university administrator, and Air Force Reserve colonel. He has a gift for storytelling and a writing style that pulls the reader into the story. He also has a knack for knowing what interests people.

This little book bears that out.

Marshall Trimble
Official Arizona State Historian

Introduction

This collection of stories about Arizona's colorful past may, I hope, convince the reader that history need not be dull. These "Arizona Nuggets" are about fascinating *people* – their triumphs and tragedies, their sorrows and their joys. You'll find few dates or statistics or footnotes in these tales, but you *will* get a better idea of what life was like on the frontier and how some of today's most cherished institutions and traditions came to be.

The collection is divided into eight sections:

In "Celebrating Arizona's Century of Statehood" we include six stories which trace some of the episodes of the long journey from the creation of Arizona Territory in 1863 to the entry of Arizona into statehood in 1912.

In the "Early Days – Pre-Territorial" section we get a glimpse of Native American life before the white man came. Here, also, are stories of the Spanish appearance on the scene; the adventures of mountain men and beaver trappers; Arizona's storied Civil War battle, and more.

In "Territorial Days" we share the incredible discomforts of riding the Butterfield Stage; the hilarious follies of a territorial legislature; the thrill of greeting the first trains which linked this isolated backwater to the rest of the world; and the terrors of braving the raging Colorado River in the first expedition through the Grand Canyon.

"Conflicts" brings the reader face to face with rival clans in the bloody Pleasant Valley War; the tragedy of the internment of loyal Japanese-Americans after Pearl Harbor; the little known impact of the Zimmermann Telegram which gave America the final push into World War I; and the historic infantry trek of the Mormon Battalion.

In the "Politics" section we help celebrate the climax of Arizona's 49-year fight for statehood; learn of the former public idol who became probably Arizona Territory's worst governor; the legacies of Carl Hayden, Ernest McFarland and Barry Goldwater; and John Rhodes' amazing upset victory in his campaign for a seat in the U.S. House of Representatives.

"Characters" is an improbable assortment of tales about some of the most fascinating personalities in western American history. You'll learn about the man who killed Santa Claus; Arizona's most celebrated liar; the swindler who became The Baron of Arizona; and the accident that brought TV star Ladmo to Phoenix.

You will learn in "Women" that a host of strong-willed females played major roles in the development of the state; that there were both angels and bad girls throughout Arizona history; that the Trunk Murderess may not have been guilty of all she was accused of in the state's most lurid murder trial; and that Yuma's first citizen was a 6'-2" bar- brawling woman who was adored by sick and wounded soldiers of two wars.

Finally, in "This and That", we wrap up everything else that doesn't fit in the other sections. When "Oklahoma!" came to Arizona, for example. The unbelievable home remedies that our sick and wounded pioneers relied on. Why Zane Grey left Arizona in a snit, never to return. And the agonizing birth of the University of Arizona.

All these are products of my nearly half-century of interviewing, research and writing about my adopted state. If you are looking for a comprehensive history of Arizona – this ain't it. I've listed some of the authoritative books and documents in the appendix that I used extensively, any one of which I recommend to you for more comprehensive and scholarly reading. But this little book? It has some instructional value, but mainly it's just to be enjoyed.

Dean Smith

Celebrating Arizona's Century of Statehood

In this special edition of *Arizona Nuggets*, we want to shine the spotlight of history on a very special event: The Centennial of Arizona statehood, celebrated throughout 2012. The Centennial marks the 100th anniversary of the day – February 14, 2012 – President William Howard Taft signed the proclamation that made Arizona the 48th state of the American Union. Stories in this section will describe the long and seemingly endless battles fought by Arizonans over nearly half a century of second-class citizenship to achieve statehood.

An interesting sidelight to this saga is the fact that Arizona had two birthdays – also in February – before the big one. When New Mexico Territory was created in 1850 from land in the vast Mexican Cession, the area we now call Arizona made up the western half of that new territory. The hardy pioneers who inhabited our half found that they were isolated from the capital, Santa Fe, and suffered from lack of federal recognition. When repeated pleas for separate United States territorial status were ignored and the South formed the Confederacy, people in what was already being called Arizona welcomed President Jefferson Davis' recognition of the southwest portion of New Mexico Territory as the Confederate Territory of Arizona.

So the first Arizona, whose birthday was February 14, 1862, was Confederate.

Our second birthday came on February 24, 1863, after Union forces prevailed here, when President Abraham Lincoln signed into law the creation of Arizona Territory.

The next step – statehood – took 49 years of struggle and repeated disappointment.

But the big day of entry into the Union came at last. That story, and a quick look at today's Arizona, brings us up to date.

Lame Ducks, Oysters and Mr. Lincoln

Abraham Lincoln had the weight of the world on his shoulders on that February day in 1863. His Union armies were losing battle after major battle. The death and injury tolls were tearing the heart out of a weary nation, and Robert E. Lee's seemingly invincible forces were preparing to launch an offensive that would reach a thunderous climax at Gettysburg not many weeks away.

Certainly the question of separate territorial status for far-off Arizona was not much on his tortured mind. But somehow he found a spare moment to sign into law a document dividing the vast New Mexico Territory in half and creating Arizona Territory.

That act, so vital to the eventual attainment of statehood for Arizonans, came about in a highly unusual way. A small group of Arizonans, including Charles Poston and General Sam Heintzelman, journeyed to Washington in December of 1862 and managed to convince a covey of recently-defeated Congressmen – Lame Ducks – that they should push for passage of the act and then go west as officials of the new territory.

At an oyster supper, a rare wartime treat, the Arizonans entertained the Lame Ducks, finalized the plan, and even drew up a slate of officials for the new territory. Ohio Congressman John Gurley was to be the first governor, but he died before the party of officials left for the wilds of Arizona. So John Goodwin of Maine took his place.

It is doubtful that President Lincoln spent much time or energy on the pros and cons of the act. But he was told there were rich mines in Arizona which must not fall into Confederate hands. On February 24 he affixed his signature and, as Poston recalled, "launched Arizona on the political seas."

The State Without a Flag

It all started in an unlikely place: Camp Perry, Ohio, where rifle teams from all over the nation gathered each year to compete for championships. The year was 1910, and the three major actors were future Congressman Carl Hayden and his wife, Nan, and Col. Charles Harris, the team captain and soon to be Adjutant General of Arizona.

One day a group of Arizona competitors complained to Harris that most of the other teams carried the flags of their states – but Arizona had none. What could be done about it? Of course, Arizona had no state flag because it was not yet a state. That recognition was still two years in the future. Harris and Carl Hayden, both ardent riflemen, got together and drew up various designs for such a flag. They agreed that its colors should be red, yellow, copper, and blue, and that it should be a striking symbol of a vigorous new state. Harris, who fathered the idea, is usually credited with the design.

Probably with Mrs. Hayden looking over their shoulders, the two amateur designers decided on a flag virtually the same as the one we honor today.

The 13 rays of the setting sun, emblematic of the West, were in red and yellow, the colors of the banners carried by Francisco Coronado on his 1540 entrada into Arizona. The five-pointed copper star in the middle of the flag honored Arizona's position as the nation's top producer of that metal. The lower half of the flag was Liberty Blue, the same color as that on the Stars and Stripes.

Not every member of the new Arizona Legislature liked the design, and it was not until February, 1917 that it was officially adopted.

Nan Hayden's role in this drama? It was she who stitched the first flag together and thus earned the title of "The Betsy Ross of Arizona."

Why 49 Years to Statehood

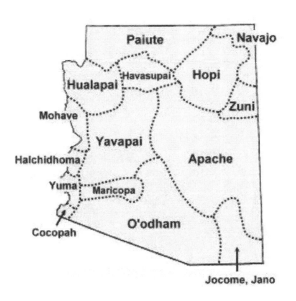

Arizona had been a separate territory for scarcely a decade before ambitious dreamers began planning for statehood. They had only to look at the successes of their neighbors to envision how short a time some territories needed to become states. Nevada, for example, made it in 1864, Colorado in 1876, and Utah in 1896. And, of course, California and Texas joined the Union without ever being territories at all.

But Arizona had special problems. It was so very remote, nearly without roads, and lightly inhabited except by fierce Indian tribes – especially Apaches – whose atrocities against settlers were eagerly reported by the eastern press. General Sherman, who visited Arizona in the 1870s, did not help when he declared that "We fought the Mexicans to get Arizona, and now we should fight them again to take it back."

Still, as the population grew and the Indian threat subsided, Arizona delegations kept descending on Washington to plead for statehood. In 1891 Arizona leaders assembled a convention, wrote a constitution, and presented it to Congress – with no success. In 1901, they persuaded President McKinley to come see for himself how far Arizona had progressed. Not long thereafter Congress proposed that Arizona and New Mexico be admitted as one state, with Santa Fe as the capital. Furious Arizonans went to the polls and buried that scheme.

Most of the barriers to statehood had been torn down by that time, but one remained: Solidly Republican administrations in Washington knew that Arizona would likely send two Democrats to the Senate. It was not until 1910 that Congress passed the Enabling Act that put Arizona on track to write a constitution and prepare to become a state. But there were more delays ahead – almost two fretful years of them.

Getting Around President Taft

Three-hundred-pound William Howard Taft was a President with solidly conservative views about government. He cherished the old ways and viewed with alarm the populist wave that was sweeping the western states and territories. These radicals, he believed, wanted the common people to have a louder voice and supported such measures as voter initiatives, referring laws back to the electorate for approval, and the worst of all in his view: popular recall of elected officials.

So it was with trepidation that Mr. Taft read the names of the 52 delegates to Arizona's Constitutional Convention. Forty-one were Democrats (mostly progressives) and only eleven were Republicans. George W. P. Hunt, the president, was as populist as they came.

For sixty days they wrangled in the hot early fall, without air conditioning, and produced a document just as objectionable as Taft had feared. He managed to swallow most of the newfangled provisions, but drew the line at allowing voters to recall judges. He sent the document back and called for another election to exclude the offending measure. So judicial recall was removed and the revised constitution was approved in the ensuing election by a wide margin. Only one Republican delegate to the convention had been willing to sign it.

Oh, yes – the new state legislature, in one of its first acts, snubbed its nose at Taft and put popular recall of judges right back into the Arizona Constitution.

Statehood – At Last!

Arizonans had waited so very long, since 1850 when Arizona had been admitted to the Union as the western half of New Mexico Territory, and then since 1863 when it became Arizona Territory. Now on that glorious day, February 14, 1912, it was about to join the Union as the 48th state.

Statehood should have come in 1911, but President Taft had refused to accept Arizona's new constitution because it provided for the election and recall of judges. Arizonans cleared that hurdle by voting to eliminate the offending provision. Statehood was then supposed to become official on February 12, 1912, but that was Lincoln's birthday, a federal holiday. The next day Taft postponed it again, claiming it was unlucky to admit a state on the 13th of the month.

So the long-awaited festivities began on the morning of February 14, when Taft at last signed the statehood document. All across the new state fireworks crackled, bells rang, parades began, and whiskey flowed. In Phoenix, a bride and groom had delayed their wedding until the signing was official, wanting to be the first couple married in the 48th state. (Their ring bearer was a 3-year old named Barry Goldwater).

Governor George W. P. Hunt, a 300-pound hulk of a man, walked more than a mile from the Ford Hotel in downtown Phoenix to the capitol building, huffing and puffing all the way, to make his inaugural address. Famed William Jennings Bryan then spoke for a seemingly endless two hours. A cannon boomed, beginning what was supposed to be a 48-gun salute, but it had to be halted after 38 salvos because horses were rearing in terror and windows were breaking. Peace descended at last, and Arizona's big day was over.

Look at Arizona Today!

It's hard to believe that the new little orphan state of 1912 has blossomed during the past century into today's super-modern, high-tech, future-oriented Arizona. As recently as 1945, the state had so few people that we had only a single member in the U. S. House of Representatives. Now we have eight and soon will have more. The 2010 U.S. census revealed that the population has skyrocketed to 6.4 million.

Arizona's economy, once limited primarily to the Five C's (copper, cattle, cotton, climate, and citrus) has expanded to electronics, tourism, sophisticated research and countless other enterprises. Phoenix now ranks as the sixth-largest city in the nation. Tucson is a metropolis and Mesa is larger than Atlanta, Cleveland or Tulsa.

And sports? Phoenix is one of only a handful of American cities that host teams in every major professional sport. Both the University of Arizona and Arizona State University are members of the elite PAC-12 Conference. The Tostitos Fiesta Bowl and the Insight Bowl are major college football events, and the Phoenix Open golf tournament is an important stop on the PGA tour.

More important are the fast-rising academic reputations of Arizona's three state universities. The U of A and ASU, along with Northern Arizona University, have earned national acclaim for their research achievements.

Quality of life has advanced along with growth. The state's fine arts institutions are a source of pride, as are the many internationally-known hotels and resorts. The quality of today's schools, residential housing, churches, and scores of other amenities help draw visitors and new residents to Arizona.

Like every other state, Arizona has struggled through the difficult days of the current economic recession. But the promises of better times to come are becoming more evident with each passing day.

Arizona enters its second century with supreme confidence.

Early Days – Pre Territorial

Some casual students of Arizona history may believe that the story began with the arrival of Marcos de Niza and Coronado in 1539-40. But in truth, the Spaniards were late comers. We now have evidence that people lived and labored and loved here at least 11,000 years ago. They hunted mammoths in those long ago days, and fashioned tools and weapons to survive. Much later, the people we call the Anasazi and the Ho-ho-kam thrived on the deserts and in the mountains. For a thousand years they remained, leaving behind them the ruins of their communities and artistic achievements.

To many of our earliest Arizona settlers, "the only good Indian is a dead Indian" was a saying too often accepted as gospel truth. But the ferocious efforts of the original inhabitants to stem the overwhelming tide of white settlement are more easily understood when one realizes that their world was rapidly collapsing and they were being penned up in reservations. Chief Cochise, whose story is told in this section, symbolizes the efforts of some Indian leaders to find a way to live peacefully with their new neighbors. Those efforts were often swept aside by the white man, who considered the Indians as merely obstacles to civilizing and developing this frontier land.

Most of what we now call Arizona was added to the Union as the western half of New Mexico Territory, in 1850 after it was ceded by Mexico. The southern quarter of our present state, including Tucson and several other towns, was acquired in the Gadsden Purchase of 1854. Nine years later, not long before the Civil War battle of Gettysburg, President Lincoln signed the document creating Arizona Territory. The new governor immediately arranged for a territorial census, which disclosed that only 4,573 inhabitants (excluding Indians) lived here. That's fewer than a third of the people who watch a Phoenix Suns basketball game today. It was on that precariously small base that modern Arizona was built.

Most of the pre-territorial citizens came to prospect for gold. Some found it, and others were enriched by silver discoveries. Copper, the heart of Arizona's economy in later years, spawned a host of mining camps when the precious metals ran out. Ranching became an economic pillar in the later 19th century.

We owe a huge debt of gratitude to those stalwarts who labored to build a foundation for the future in those pre-territorial years: Father Kino, who came to Christianize the natives and teach them how to raise crops and live more productive lives; Charles Poston, who earned the title "Father of Arizona" for his efforts to create the new territory and start it on its way; Charles Hayden and Michel Goldwater, the Zeckendorf brothers and other pioneer entrepreneurs; and the sturdy women who bore the children and braved the dangers and discomforts of the raw frontier.

Pattie: Arizona's First American Chronicler

James Ohio Pattie may have been the first American to enter what is now Arizona. He certainly was the first to write a book about it.

In 1825 he and several other young adventurers crossed Republic of Mexico territory, from Santa Fe to San Diego. Arizona at that time was unnamed and virtually unpopulated, except by a few Mexican soldiers and priests, and hordes of warlike Indians who were determined to chase the buckskin-clad Americans off their homeland.

Why did Pattie's party come to such a forbidding place? Not for gold or silver, but for beaver pelts, which were much in demand by the fur hat wearers of the eastern states. Arizona's rivers were teeming with beavers at that time and the Pattie party trapped in almost all of them – the Gila (James called it the "Hee-lay"), the San Pedro, the San Francisco, and the Salt.

Indians stole their horses and forced the trappers to walk back to New Mexico. Returning to Arizona, they gathered more pelts than they could carry, so they hid them, planning to come back for them later. But the wily Apaches found the cache and stole the furs. Later the party trapped down the Gila River to the Salt, but all except Pattie and two others were massacred by Indians near the site of today's Phoenix.

Pattie's book, which he published in 1830 after his return home, is sprinkled with unlikely tales of killing a bear in a cave, rescuing beautiful young women who had been captured by Comanches and stripped naked, and finding 16 arrows in his bed roll after repelling an Apache attack. Such gilding of the truth was common in publications of that day, but Pattie's narrative provided an accurate description of Arizona geography and wild life.

A sad postscript: The ensuing invasion of trappers all but wiped out the beaver population in Arizona rivers in little more than a decade.

Lt. Ives' Bad Guess

If there is a Guinness Book of Records category for the worst prediction, that honor certainly belongs to Lt. Joseph Ives.

It was in 1858 that the young army officer was chosen to explore the navigability of the Colorado River north of the town we now know as Yuma. In an unwieldy stern- paddled steamboat called *The Explorer,* he and his crew battled the swift current as far north as today's Hoover Dam. There he left the boat for a time and made his way with native guides up to the Grand Canyon, which was at that time virtually unknown except to the Indians. He snaked his way to the river below, thus becoming the first white man to perform that feat.

Lt. Ives was not much impressed by what is now called one of the Seven Wonders of the World. In his report he made this amazing observation:

"It can be approached only from the south, and after entering it there is nothing to do but leave. Ours has been the first, and doubtless the last, party of whites to visit this profitless locality."

Talk about bad predictions! It's too bad that Ives cannot come back a century and a half later to mingle with the more than three million Grand Canyon visitors from every corner of the earth who come every year to marvel at this awesome work of nature.

Saintly Father Kino

Who was this amazing Father Kino, whose statue stands in the U.S. Capitol rotunda – who laid the foundations of the famed San Xavier del Bac mission church nine miles south of Tucson – the explorer who discovered that Baja California was not an island – and who gave up a life of ease in Italy to minister to the primitive Indians of southern Arizona? Born Eusebio Chino in 1645, he promised God at age 18 that he would be a missionary if he survived a near-fatal illness. He longed to serve in east Asia, but his Jesuit superiors sent him instead to what is now Arizona, at that time a barely explored desert virtually untouched by Europeans.

Because Chino meant "Chinaman" in Spanish, he changed his name to "Kino" shortly after his arrival in Mexico. He and a few brother monks started to build a chain of missions in northern Sonora and southern Arizona, teaching the Pimas and other Indians the arts of farming and ranching, and introducing cattle and horses to the area. So appreciative were the natives that they soon idolized Father Kino and many hundreds became Christians.

Whenever he could, he went on exploration trips, discovering the ancient Casa Grande structure near today's Coolidge, and venturing north to the Gila River and modern Tempe. Two of the Arizona missions he established, Tumacacori and San Xavier, still exist. The beautiful San Xavier church – fondly known as "The White Dove of the Desert" – was completed long after his death at age 66 in 1711 but it stands today as a memorial to the dedicated missionary who brought civilization to Arizona.

13

The Odd Couple

They were as different as two men could be: Estevan, the African slave – young, huge, athletic, and egotistical; and Marcos de Niza, the grizzled old Franciscan priest – small in stature, slow and deliberate, humble and pious. The viceroy of New Spain had cast them together for an historic exploration of the Terra Incognita, the mysterious land we now know as Arizona and New Mexico. They departed with high hopes, little suspecting that both would die tragically within a few months.

In March of 1539 they led a small party northward from Mexico City to investigate exciting rumors of fabulous riches in the Seven Cities of Cibola, where streets were said to be paved with gold. Estevan, impatient with Marcos' plodding pace, soon took off on his own, promising to send back messengers with word about what lay ahead. Once free of Marcos' restraint, he played the role of a medicine man, dancing, coloring his body with gaudy paints, and draping feathers about his shoulders. His act apparently wowed the Indian maidens along the way, and they flocked to him in droves. But the men of the Pueblo villages were so offended by Estevan's antics that they promptly killed and dismembered him. However, the boisterous show-off had earned a place in history as the first non-Indian to set foot on Arizona soil.

When Marcos learned of the slave's murder, he made preparations to flee back to New Spain. He was in sight of the village of Hawikuh near the Arizona-New Mexico border and saw its adobe huts at sunset, when the glow apparently convinced him that they were made of gold. Once back home, he let his imagination run wild, reporting to the viceroy that he had seen cities larger and richer than Mexico City. Excitement reigned as a young nobleman named Francisco Vasquez de Coronado assembled an army of gold-hungry men to march northward in search of fame and wealth.

Marcos, of course, was chosen to guide them. When the conquering heroes reached Hawikuh and found it to be a squalid village with not an ounce of gold, the enraged Coronado gave Marcos the tongue-lashing of his life and sent him home in disgrace. So dispirited was the old priest that he suffered a stroke and died soon after his arrival.

14

When the Meteor Struck Arizona

Fifty thousand years ago, give or take a few months, a white-hot fireball roared down from space and collided with our Earth in northern Arizona, between Flagstaff and Winslow, five miles south of Interstate 40. It struck with devastating force, creating a crater in the high desert almost a mile across and deep enough to hide the Washington Monument. It is the largest object from space ever to land in the United States.

A visitor to its rim, awed by the chasm below, once declared: "Man! It's a lucky thing that meteor didn't hit the freeway!"

For many decades, Meteor Crater was thought to have been caused by a volcano, but a stubborn Philadelphian named Daniel Barringer was convinced that a meteor was responsible. He spent much of his considerable fortune and many years in excavating the floor of the crater, so certain was he that a large mass of iron must be somewhere beneath its floor. He never found the rich metal ball, but he did discover many hundreds of large meteorites on and near the site, proving at last that the crater was created by a huge meteor. What happened to the main mass of the fireball? Scientists now agree that most of it evaporated in the intense heat of the collision.

Today visitors flock to Meteor Crater from all over the world. They see where American astronauts trained for the first moon landing, view films about the crater in a spacious theater, marvel at the meteorites in the museum, and spend money in the gift shop. A private corporation, Meteor Crater Enterprises, manages the crater facilities. It's well worth a day's trip to see Meteor Crater for yourself.

The Jackass Mail

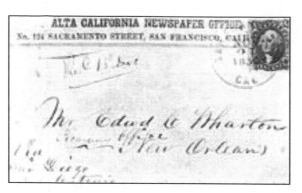

Its real name was "The San Antonio and San Diego Mail Line," but Arizona pioneers loved to call it "The Jackass Mail" because its coaches were pulled by mules. Arizona's first passenger and mail service was launched in July, 1857–a year before the better-remembered Butterfield Overland Mail began operation. Advertised as "an armed escort through the Indian country," it left San Antonio and San Diego twice each month.

The trip through Texas, New Mexico, Arizona and California took 26 days. It was a grueling adventure for even the most hardy passenger, with few amenities, abominable food and cramped lodgings. The advent of the Butterfield line doomed the Jackass Mail, and it was terminated in 1858.

Cochise: A Respected Apache Chief

Sorrowfully, they dressed him in his best attire, with his prize rifle at his side. They killed his horse and buried it with him so that he could ride in the spirit world. Then his fellow Apaches covered the grave in his beloved Dragoon Mountains and kept its location secret – and secret it remains to this day. Cochise? Newcomers to Arizona may never have heard of this great Chiricahua Apache chief, one of the most prominent figures in early Arizona history. Much as they feared him, his white contemporaries respected his valor, his honesty and his longing for peace. He is the only Native American to have his name on an Arizona county. Born in what is now southeast Arizona in 1812, he fought bravely to keep his people free until his death in 1874.

"You must speak straight so that your words may go as sunlight into our hearts," he once declared. "Speak, Americans. I will not lie to you; do not lie to me." But most white invaders of Apacheland believed that "the only good Indian is a dead Indian" and lied to Cochise at every turn. They trampled on treaties and, when the Apaches struck back, they killed the outnumbered natives or penned them up in reservations.

Cochise, a remarkably fluent speaker, bared his soul to his white friend Thomas Jeffords: "Nobody wants peace more than I do. Why shut me up on a reservation? We will make peace and keep it faithfully. But let us go free as Americans do. Let us go where we please." But there would be no peace. Hotheads such as the young Geronimo wanted only to kill the invaders and they did so, in horrible ways. In the end the last free Apaches, led by Geronimo, surrendered in 1886 and were exiled to Florida.

Arizona at 39 Cents an Acre

ARIZONA

Gadsden Purchase
1854

MEXICO

One of Arizona's favorite legends blames its slanting southern border on surveyors who got thirsty and headed northwest to the nearest saloon, in Yuma. But, sadly, it just isn't true.

The nearly 30,000 square miles of the 1854 Gadsden Purchase – all of Arizona south of the Gila River and the tip of southwest New Mexico – slants up from Nogales to just south of Yuma because Mexican dictator Santa Anna refused to give up a land bridge that connects Baja California to the rest of Mexico.

James Gadsden of South Carolina, as fiery a southern rebel who ever lived, was chosen by President Franklin Pierce and Secretary of War Jefferson Davis to go to Mexico City and buy land for a southern railway to the Pacific (and, incidentally, add a huge piece of territory to what would soon be the Confederacy). Gadsden first offered to buy most of the tier of northern Mexican states for $50 million. Santa Anna, who desperately needed money to put down a fomenting revolution, was tempted to accept. But he didn't.

Gadsden then proposed three smaller purchases, all of which would have given Arizona a seaport on the Gulf of California, but without success. Finally, he and the Mexicans agreed on a deal: No gulf port, and a price of only $15 million.

The U.S. Senate, with northerners bitterly opposed, finally accepted the deal, but only for $10 million. That figures out at about 39 cents an acre – certainly one of the best real estate purchases of all time. Mexico was in no position to quibble. Early in the morning after the Gadsden Treaty was approved, an eager Mexican official was waiting at the door of the U.S. Treasury to collect.

Poston's Little Heaven on Earth

It was in 1856 – two years after James Gadsden bought southern Arizona from Mexico – that Charles Poston established himself as ruler of the land surrounding the former presidio of Tubac and created his own little Garden of Eden there. It was theoretically governed from Santa Fe, the capital of New Mexico Territory, but Tubac was so remote from U.S. authority that nobody bothered to interfere. Poston's nearby silver mine attracted more than eight hundred residents to the community, most of them from Sonora, and it paid for food, other necessities, and many luxuries, as well.

"We had no law but love," Poston later wrote. "I was authorized to celebrate the rites of matrimony, baptize children, grant divorces, execute criminals, and declare war."

While the newcomers did all the manual labor, Poston was free to relax in the shade by the Santa Cruz River and to read, drink fine wines, and smoke expensive cigars. Because the Mexican miners could not read English, Poston created paper money printed with pictures of animals to indicate the various denominations.

Before many months had passed, a Catholic cleric from Santa Fe paid a visit and was horrified to learn that Tubac weddings had not been sanctified by a priest. He thus declared all the marriages null and void. This created panic in the community, but Poston persuaded the visiting padre to declare the unions legal by paying him $700.

By 1860, Apache raids and the approach of the Civil War brought an end to Poston's paradise and he devoted all his considerable talents toward the creation of a separate Arizona Territory. He led a delegation that accomplished this feat in 1863, thus earning him the title of "Father of Arizona."

The Great Camel Experiment

Secretary of War Jefferson Davis, later president of the Confederacy, had a bright idea: Why not import camels from the Sahara Desert to haul freight and military supplies across the Arizona desert to California? So he sent envoys to North Africa in 1856 to bring back 74 of the ungainly beasts for a trial run. Lt. Ned Beale's 1857 trek in search of a railroad route or wagon road across northern Arizona was the first to employ them.

At first the camels seemed the ideal vehicles for the task. They could carry a thousand-pound load – enough to crush a mule – for 65 miles in a single day. Moreover, they could go without water for three days and would eat virtually any wild bush along the way. But troubles appeared almost at the outset. They required imported Arab drivers to keep them under control ("They never learned English!" one Arab explained) and they caused the terrified mules and horses to lay back their ears and race off into the desert.

Moreover, they tended to bite any man or beast who came near, and their breath was foul enough to send a man into convulsions. Within a few months, the great experiment ended in failure and the Army released the camels to roam away at will.

For a hundred years or more, reports of wild camel sightings were common, and some folks claim they are still out there today. Only one Arab camel driver – Hadji Ali – known to all as "Hi Jolly" remained until his death in 1902. Visitors to Quartzsite, near the Colorado River, can see the pyramid tomb with a camel on top, erected in Hi Jolly's memory.

The Casa Grande – Fascinating!

It was a gathering of experts not to be matched in Arizona for centuries to come — construction engineers, artisans, irrigation pioneers, astronomers, farmers, musicians, and many others. They learned to tame the desert and thrived for more than a thousand years before they mysteriously disappeared in the early 1400s. The remains of ball courts testify to their love of sports, and Mexican mirrors and copper bells reveal that they were long-ranging traders.

These people, whom we know as the Ho-ho-kam, built a community just outside present-day Coolidge, and its amazing "skyscraper," the four-story Big House, has survived to this day. In 1892 the Casa Grande, as early Spanish explorers called it, became the first edifice in America to be protected as an archeological preserve, and now has the status of a national monument.

It is an engineering marvel, constructed in layers of caliche adobe, with walls four feet thick at the base and tapering toward the top. For the interior rooms, hundreds of pine, juniper and fir trees were carried or floated down the Gila River some sixty miles from the mountain forests. The Big House was so sturdily constructed that it has withstood the ravages of time and weather for at least seven centuries.

Why was it built? It is believed that it was used as a fort, a gathering place, a temple of worship, and an astronomical observatory. Small holes in the walls were aligned so that the sun's rays would pass through to signal the beginning of the seasons. The scientific knowledge and advanced culture of the Ho-ho-kam — too soon forgotten by later generations – remains a subject of wonder for us all.

Coronado: Magnificent Failure

He led the small army that opened up the American Southwest to the world. His name graces cities, schools, geographical features, and a national forest. But Francisco Vasquez de Coronado never knew much fame during his short life, and died in disgrace and obscurity.

It all started in 1539, when Fray Marcos de Niza returned to New Spain (Mexico) with a glowing report of golden cities in the lands to the north. Coronado was chosen to lead the expedition of conquest, and 350 eager young men signed up to seek their fortunes in the uncharted Terra Incognita we now call Arizona and New Mexico. In early 1540, with Marcos leading the way, they hurried up the San Pedro River valley, past today's Benson, Arizona, and trekked northeastward toward the present site of Albuquerque. En route, they entered the Hawikah pueblo which Marcos had raved about and found only half-starved Indians – but not one iota of gold. Coronado surely would have killed Marcos had he not been a priest, but gave him only a tongue lashing and sent him back to Mexico City in disgrace.

The Coronado army camped on the site of Albuquerque for a year, ranging east and west in a vain search for riches. They discovered the awesome Grand Canyon, the verdant valley of the Rio Grande, and scores of pueblos, mapping the territory and recording their findings for posterity. Then they ranged eastward, encountering mammoth herds of bison in west Texas and Indian tribes in Kansas before giving up their search for gold.

When he returned to Mexico City, ragged and crestfallen, Coronado was branded as an abject failure and was soon forgotten. He died in 1554, aged 44, and the location of his burial place was forgotten for three centuries – until persistent scholars located it at last in Mexico City's Santo Domingo Church.

The Peddler of Gila City

Mining towns sprang up like dandelions in mid-19th century Arizona, and they withered and died almost as rapidly. Such was the case of Gila City, a rowdy amalgamation of fortune hunters, cutthroats, ladies of the evening, and gamblers, 18 miles east of Yuma on the Gila River.

Roving reporter J. Ross Browne filed this colorful description of the new town in 1860: "Gila City has over a thousand hardy adventurers prospecting the gulches and canyons for gold. Enterprising men hurried to the spot with barrels of whiskey and billiard tables. Jews came with ready-made clothing and fancy wares, and gamblers came with cards and monte tables. There was everything in Gila City within a few months but a church and a jail, which were regarded as barbarisms by the mass of the population."

One of those Jewish peddlers was none other than Michel Goldwater, Barry's grandfather. He entered what is now Arizona in 1860, driving a borrowed mule-drawn wagon piled high with trade goods, which he soon sold at a good profit to the eager miners. "Big Mike" had come to America from London eight years before and opened a saloon at Sonora, Calif. That failed venture plunged him into bankruptcy and reduced him to scratching out a living as a peddler.

With his Gila City profits he opened a store at La Paz, Arizona, and another at Ehrenberg, across the Colorado River from today's Blythe, Calif. Neither store was very profitable, so he moved on to open another at Prescott. That store, selling everything from mining equipment to ladies' vanities, was a success.

But the first real Goldwater money maker was the Phoenix store opened by his son Baron in 1896 – the first in Arizona to cater primarily to ladies in higher income brackets. By that time the Gila City peddler had retired and spent his sunset years in San Francisco.

23

The Butterfield Stage: Hell on Wheels

So you think it has gotten to be a hassle to fly to California? Just be glad you never had to trek westward across Arizona on the Butterfield Stage. After such a bone-jolting ride in 1858 a weary passenger had this to say about it: "Imagine three on a seat, knees locked together. A sardine canner would have gone mad with envy. Racing along the rough trail we would solemnly rise from our seats, bump our heads against the low roof, and return in unison once more. All the time the hoofs of the galloping horses kicked a perpetual cloud of dust into our faces and sleep was all but impossible."

To maximize revenue, the management crammed nine or more passengers into the coach, and often had three others clinging precariously to the roof. Each was permitted 40 pounds of luggage and mail bags were crammed in somehow. There were no Motel Sixes or McDonalds in that race across southern New Mexico (now Arizona) Territory, and the company had to complete each St. Louis-to-San Francisco trek in 25 days. So there were no sleep stops, and only 20 to 30 minutes to wolf down beans and jerked beef at the meal stops. All the while, nervous drivers kept a lookout for raiding Apaches, who sometimes stole the horses and either killed the passengers or left them stranded on the burning desert.

John Butterfield performed a miracle in creating his stage company, spending a million dollars in less than a year to hire 800 men, acquire 250 Concord coaches and 1800 horses, and equip 139 relay stations over the 2,812-mile route. But the Pony Express took over most of the mail business in 1859 and the onset of the Civil War in 1861 forced Butterfield to discontinue his southern route. When the coaches and the military presence disappeared, the jubilant Apaches – convinced that they had chased the white man away – descended on the helpless settlers and all but depopulated Arizona.

The Civil War's Westernmost Battle?

Picacho Peak, forty miles north of Tucson, was for thirty minutes on April 12, 1862 a scene of desperate hand-to-hand conflict which has gone down in history as the westernmost battle of the Civil War. Here on this rocky promontory a detachment of Union cavalry clashed in a mortal struggle with Rebel defenders who were determined to open a path for Confederate dominance of the Southwest and California.

With President Jefferson Davis' blessing, Colonel John Baylor had declared much of today's New Mexico and Arizona as the "Confederate Territory of Arizona." Tucson, the only town of consequence in that area, was occupied by the Confederates and Southern California was dominated by southern sympathizers. Only a bold move by a Union force could thwart the Rebel ambitions. That force, 1,500 men led by Col. James Carleton and christened "The California Column," raced down from northern California in early 1862 and prepared for a clash with the Rebels.

En route, a small enemy party fired on the Californians at Stanwix Station, eighty miles east of Yuma, and a Union private was wounded before the two bands of combatants broke off the brief action. This skirmish could, therefore, be called the westernmost battle of the war.

When the Californians reached what is now the outskirts of Chandler, Lt. James Barrett led a small party on a reconnaissance mission and encountered the Rebels ensconced on Picacho Peak. Bullets flew, Barrett and two Union enlisted men were killed, men on both sides were wounded, and three Confederates were taken prisoner. Greatly outnumbered, the Rebel force left Tucson in a hurry and retreated back to Texas, never to threaten the Southwest again.

Arizona's two brief moments in the annals of the Civil War were at an end.

Territorial Days

Early residents of Arizona Territory longed for statehood, but it was a long time coming – 49 years, to be exact. In contrast to neighboring California and Nevada, both of which had joined the Union as states before the end of 1864, Arizona labored under several almost insurmountable handicaps. Foremost was the Indian problem, which kept all but the most adventuresome from risking their families' lives here until the last Apaches laid down their weapons in 1886. Population grew at a snail's pace, leading Washington bigwigs to ignore the pleas of the few who sought to join the Union. The territory's remoteness from the nation's centers of activity was a problem, as was the desert heat, untamed by air conditioning.

But, small and remote as it was, Arizona enjoyed some of its most memorable history during that long period between the formation of the territory in 1863 and becoming the 48th state in 1912. This was the era of the cowboy, of gun fights in rustic saloons, of the advent of the railroad and the first automobiles, founding of the universities, and the birth of cities which became major population centers. The seat of territorial government see-sawed between Prescott and Tucson before Phoenix captured it for good in 1889, and some of the West's most outrageous political shenanigans took place in those not-so-hallowed halls.

Arizona sent emissaries to Washington year after year to plead for statehood, but in vain. Finally, in 1901, President McKinley came to the territory to see for himself whether we were worthy, but he left after a brief visit, unconvinced that we were ready.

An abortive proposal to grant statehood to a giant hunk of land composed of both New Mexico and Arizona was considered a few years later. New Mexico was heartily in favor, since the new state capital would be Santa Fe, but Arizonans rebelled. It was not until 1911, the year Roosevelt Dam was completed and Phoenix's economic future was therefore assured, that President Taft signed an enabling act that put Arizona statehood on the fast track. On the morning of February 14, 1912, the great news of "statehood at last!" was flashed over the telegraph wires and Arizonans' wild celebrations began.

Just How Tough Was Tombstone?

When Ed Schieffelin told Fort Huachuca soldiers one day in 1877 that he was going to prospect for silver in the heart of Apache country, one of them snorted "All you're going to find out there is your own tombstone!" Ed remembered that warning when he discovered the richest silver lode in Arizona history and named his town. Soon Tombstone became a beehive of activity, swarming with miners, saloon keepers, gun slingers, gamblers, prostitutes, and cutthroats of every stripe. Its fame as the toughest and most sinful town in the Southwest spread from coast to coast.

How tough was it? Bob Boze Bell, publisher of "True West" magazine, decided to find out, and buried himself for days among the crumbling pages of the 1881 *Tombstone Epitaph* in the archives of ASU's Hayden Library. Sure enough, he found plenty of evidence of the town's toughness in that pioneer newspaper – stories of murders, thievery and swindles, topped off by the famed Gunfight at the OK Corral.

But what surprised him were the advertisements for Tombstone's leading emporiums. Four coffee bars were flourishing, along with a wine parlor catering to ladies. The Birdcage Theater offered concerts and theater performances by some of the nation's top stars. Latest feminine finery was advertised.

On rowdy Allen Street, the Earps and Clantons must have passed right by – amazingly – an ice cream parlor, on their way to their bloody battle near the OK Corral. One of the biggest surprises was a directory of Tombstone telephones. More than a dozen of them were in use in 1881, only five years after their invention by Alexander Graham Bell.

Maybe Tombstone was a bit more civilized than we thought.

Geronimo: Devil or Hero?

His only regret, Geronimo told a biographer in his later years, was that he did not die in the Sierra Madre mountains, fighting the hated white soldiers. But to another writer, he added a second regret: that he had caused so much pain to little children. "After raiding a ranch and killing the father and mother," he said ruefully, "I would take the little ones out of their cradles and impale them on my knife until they were dead."

The most famous of all southwestern Indian warriors was unbelievably cruel, but brave and clever as well. He and some forty other Chiricahua Apache tribesmen somehow evaded 5,000 American soldiers and 3,000 Mexican pursuers for more than a year during 1885-86, killing more than 500 white settlers and winning the adoration of his people. Geronimo was the last Indian leader to surrender, giving himself up to General Nelson Miles at Skeleton Canyon in southeastern Arizona on September 8, 1886.

Geronimo's hatred of whites stemmed from an evening in 1858 when he returned home to find that Mexican soldiers had raided the Apache camp, carried off the young women, and murdered Geronimo's wife, mother and three children. He dreamed that night that he had been given supernatural powers and that he could not be killed by bullets. He became a medicine man, although never (as popularly believed) a chief.

When Geronimo surrendered, he was promised that he could return to Arizona after two years' incarceration in Florida. But that promise was broken, and he never saw his homeland again. In 1905, when he was nearly 80, he pleaded with President Teddy Roosevelt to be released. But Arizonans still had too much fear and hatred of him. Roosevelt reluctantly said "no" and Geronimo died at Fort Sill, Oklahoma in 1909.

Who Were the Sub-Normals?

There were no high schools in Arizona Territory in 1886, when the Territorial Normal School (now ASU) first opened its doors, and there would be none for more than a decade later. So it made good sense for the Normal to include among its students a Preparatory Class, teaching high school subjects and preparing students for entry into the regular curriculum.

These youngsters, most in their early teens, were officially designated as "Sub-Normals." They were welcomed by the Normal Board of Education because the tuition they paid was a sizable percentage of each annual budget.

The practice of admitting students without high school diplomas was short-lived at the Tempe institution. In 1898 a group of Normal students petitioned the governing board to discontinue the Preparatory Class, arguing that it was an embarrassment to an institution of higher learning. The board agreed, and the Sub-Normals were soon only an amusing footnote to ASU's long history.

It is interesting to note that the University of Arizona, which did not admit its first class until 1891, also had a Preparatory Class. It, too, helped balance the school budget, and there was considerable opposition to dropping the program.

It was not until 1916 that the university agreed to eliminate it.

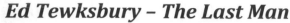

Ed Tewksbury – The Last Man

Millions have read Zane Grey's "To the Last Man," the story of the bloody Pleasant Valley War, but few know that Tom Graham was murdered by the "last man" at what is now the corner of Broadway and Priest in Tempe. Graham, in his final moments on earth, declared it was Ed Tewksbury who fired the fatal shot that ended the infamous Graham-Tewksbury feud. And it probably was. In fact, the jury in Tewksbury's first trial found him guilty, but he was freed on a technicality.

In his second trial, enough "witnesses" were rounded up by the sheep-herding Tewksbury clan to deadlock the jury and Ed was freed. His friend John Rhodes was with Ed at the time of the shooting and may have fired moments later. But Rhodes was never convicted, and lived until 1918.

The feud between cattlemen and sheepmen beneath the Mogollon Rim east of Payson boiled for ten years, claiming the lives of some forty combatants, before Tom Graham began his ill-fated wagon ride on August 2, 1892 to deliver grain to the Hayden Mill. He had left Pleasant Valley, married, bought a farm west of Tempe, and vowed never again to shoot a gun in anger.

But Ed Tewksbury, the only other survivor of the feuding, wanted vengeance. With his friend John Rhodes, he rode up behind Graham's wagon and fired a rifle bullet that severed Tom's spinal cord and left him totally paralyzed. Within hours, he was dead. It is likely that Rhodes also fired his rifle at the same moment, but in those days before ballistic analysis it was impossible to be sure which bullet ended Graham's life. There was a fascinating footnote to the case: At a preliminary hearing, Tom's distraught widow smuggled a pistol into the courtroom and tried to kill Tewksbury. But her gun jammed and Tewksbury escaped unscathed.

The Iron Horse Arrives in Tucson

The coming of the railroad to Arizona Territory opened the door to its progress more than any other event. Before the Southern Pacific's rails started creeping from Yuma eastward to Tucson in 1877, most visitors to the territory had to endure long and tortuous rides over desert terrain in horse-drawn wagons or stage coaches.

It was not until March 20, 1880 that the first railroad engine puffed and wheezed into Tucson, at that time Arizona's largest town. Its arrival was greeted with wild celebrations and ceremonies. After a silver spike was driven into the last steel rail, a band blared and politicians bombasted. Venerable Charles Poston, "The Father of Arizona," roared to the crowd, "The chariot of fire has arrived in Tucson on its way across the continent. We welcome the railroad as the Messiah of civilization."

Mayor R.N. Leatherwood decided to telegraph news of the great event to cities and dignitaries all over the nation. Someone urged him to include the Pope in Rome on his list. So Leatherwood sent word to His Holiness that "the railroad now connects us with the entire Christian world." A prankster in the telegraph office decided to fake a reply, which so excited the mayor that he assembled a crowd to hear the Pope's message.

He tore open the envelope and read, in part: "His Holiness acknowledges receipt of your telegram and sends his benediction." Leatherwood glowed – until the final sentence: "For his own satisfaction, however, he asks: WHERE THE HELL IS TUCSON?"

The Thieving Thirteenth

The 13th Arizona Territorial Legislature, which met in Prescott in February, 1885, richly deserved its nickname: The Thieving Thirteenth. When it adjourned in an alcoholic but euphoric haze, *The Tombstone Epitaph* called it "that disgraceful conglomeration of tricksters, knaves, and idiots." Many Arizona historians have used even more colorful language in describing it.

Those rollicking roisterers squandered more tax money, guzzled more whiskey, fought more fights, and infuriated more constituents than any legislature before or since. The Thirteenth exceeded its authorized budget eleven times over, and two grand juries were assembled to investigate its misdeeds.

Tucson boosters openly bribed legislators in a failed attempt to get the territorial capital moved back to their town. Proponents of creating a new county to be called Sierra Bonita doled out a small fortune, again in vain. Many of the lawmakers hired "clerks" who turned out to be family members or ladies of the evening. Excessive claims for travel reimbursements were rife, but none topped the claim of a Prescott Councilman (senator) who lived a block from the capitol but submitted a bill for travel from the Utah border. They paid newspaper publishers $17,000 for printing, in hopes that their misdeeds might be reported more leniently.

There were many reports of drunken brawls, one challenge to a duel, and a fist fight on the House floor that so terrified the sergeant at arms that he ran from the room in panic. There were few dull moments in the exciting life of the Thieving Thirteenth.

But, amazingly, its members produced some memorable legislation: the creation of both the University of Arizona and today's Arizona State University – establishment of the first Arizona hospital for the insane and the first bureau to attract settlers and tourists – funding of vital railroad building – the list goes on. They may have been thieves, drunks, and alley fighters, but their legacy to Arizona is still alive today.

Even the Sheep Said Baa-bitt.

A century ago there was a popular saying in Arizona Territory: "First God made northern Arizona, and then he turned it over to the Babbitts to run." Those five amazing brothers from Cincinnati owned cattle ranches spreading from the Grand Canyon to the New Mexico border – more sheep outfits than they could count – Indian trading posts – general stores in every town – livery stables, meat packing plants, undertaking parlors, mines, farms, ice plants, a silver fox farm, and too many other enterprises to recount here.

Three of the brothers were clever enough to marry daughters of the wealthy Verkamp family of Cincinnati, thus assuring them enough capital for multiple investments.

One cherished family legend is about the movie theater the Babbitts started in Flagstaff. In the infancy of cinema there was a short subject about a bevy of beauties starting to disrobe just as a train passed by. By the time it had passed, the girls had changed to bathing suits. One old cowhand paid to see the film five times, declaring "I know trains, and one of these times, this one will be late!"

The Babbitt saga began on a cold April 1886 morning in Flagstaff, when David and Billy stepped from a train and started looking for a cattle ranch to buy. They soon found one for sale and christened it the "CO-Bar," for Cincinnati, Ohio. The family business empire blossomed from that small beginning. Few pioneer families have been more prominent in Arizona affairs – producing state senators, county supervisors, mayors, and civic leaders of all kinds. The best known is Charles' grandson Bruce, who became attorney general and governor of Arizona, and later served as Secretary of the Interior and made a run for President.

Did a Glass Eye Change Arizona History?

Arizona's territorial capital moved around so much in the late 19th Century that historians like to refer to it as "the capital on wheels."

It all started in December, 1863 when the first governor's party arrived by covered wagons at Navajo Springs in northeast Arizona. Two weeks later they arrived at Del Rio Springs, 15 miles north of what is now Prescott, and spent seven months there before moving to Prescott. It was there, meeting in the log cabin that still stands at Sharlot Hall Museum, that the officers launched the first census (4,573 Arizona residents were counted, excluding Indians).

Tucson, the territory's largest town, had the votes to move the capital there in 1867, but Prescott reclaimed it in 1877. The seat of government remained there until 1889, when legislators from booming Phoenix campaigned to move it there. Prescott and Yavapai County fought vigorously to keep the capital, and seemed likely to win.

But the night before the proposal came to a vote in the legislature, according to a cherished Arizona legend, fate stepped in. A Prescott lawmaker who had a glass eye spent the evening with a lady of the evening in her cubicle on Whiskey Row. Before he went to sleep he put his glass eye in a tumbler of water beside the bed. The lady, it is said, got thirsty during the night and gulped down the water and the eye. Too vain to appear in the legislative session, the Prescott lawmaker refused to attend and Phoenix succeeded in capturing the capital.

By one vote, so the story goes.

Birth of the Big Game Rivalry

A screaming crowd of 300 partisans, most of whom had never seen a football game before, had no idea that they were witnessing history in the making on that 1899 Thanksgiving Day afternoon at Tucson's Carrillo Gardens. The University of Arizona team hosted the Territorial Normal School (now ASU) in the inaugural game of a rivalry that has burned fiercely for more than a century. Spectators either sat in buggies bordering the field or stood during the two-hour spectacle. The field itself had been plowed to lessen the chance of injury to the players, who wore no helmets or pads. Most were protected only by clothing stuffed inside their shirts and pants.

In those days of football's infancy there were no passes, no razzle-dazzle, and very little planned offense. When the ball was snapped the linemen formed a wedge in front of the runner and bulled their way toward the goal line. The Normals, apparently, were more muscular and pushed the University boys around to win the victory, 11-2. Normal halfback Charlie Haigler was the star of the game. He was destined to play six years for the Normal and four more for the University of Southern California.

Good sportsmanship was the rule in that far-off era. The Normal team was welcomed at the Tucson railroad station by the University players and fans, and players from both schools mingled at a sumptuous Thanksgiving feast after the game.

Football was deemed too brutal by many college presidents, so the two Arizona rivals met only sporadically for the next quarter century. During that period the University dominated the boys from Tempe, who had to wait 32 years for their second triumph over the Wildcats from Tucson.

Religion Comes to Tombstone

Most people have heard something about the Rev. Endicott Peabody – spiritual advisor for the young Franklin D. Roosevelt – founder of the famous Groton School in Massachusetts, which was attended by FDR and his four sons – the priest who officiated at the wedding of Franklin and Eleanor. But very few know that at age 25 Endicott came to Tombstone to try to tame the wild town known as the most sinful in all America.

The young cleric, not yet ordained by the Episcopal Church, had been a star athlete at England's Cambridge University, a boxer of note, and a baseball player of rare talent. When he stepped off the stage coach in Tombstone that January morning in 1882, even the most whiskey-soaked sinners and brawlers on Allen Street could see at a glance that he was a man who could handle himself against any of the bad guys in town.

Peabody's first order of business was to raise enough money to build a church. He got acquainted in a hurry, soon making friends with Wyatt Earp and many of the gamblers and bordello habitués. He toured the saloons, hat in hand, and came out with amazing amounts of folding money. Once he interrupted a high-stakes poker game, bet $50 on his first hand, and soon owned everybody's chips. He gained further respect by knocking out the miners' boxing champion.

When nobody else was brave enough to umpire a game between two bitter rival baseball teams, he agreed to take the job – but only if members of both teams would show up at church the next day. By the end of his short stay in Tombstone, he had raised enough money to build St. Paul's Church, now the oldest Protestant church in Arizona and a mecca for tourists.

A Capital on Wheels

Ask almost any long-time Arizonans to name the first capital of Arizona Territory and they will reply "Prescott." But they would be wrong.

For the first seven months of its existence, this territory was governed from a barracks room at Camp (later Fort) Whipple, a cavalry post situated some five miles north of the present town of Chino Valley. It was there, on a January day in 1864, that the weary and half frozen men of the first governor's party stumbled in from their trek across the wilderness and set up shop. It was not until August of that year that Governor John Goodwin and his associates moved into a log structure on what is now Gurley Street in the raw new town of Prescott.

That cabin, long ago destroyed, had dirt floors and was so unlivable that Goodwin invited the officers and legislators to perform their duties in the Governor's Mansion – a log house that has been preserved at Sharlot Hall Museum. Arizona's governmental center has been moved again and again – earning it the name of "The Capital on Wheels."

After only three years in Prescott, it was highjacked by Tucson legislators, who had the clout to move it to the Old Pueblo. There the legislature met at first in an adobe store building, hardly more spacious than its Prescott home. In 1877, after ten years in Tucson, the capital was moved back to Prescott. But in 1889, the rapid growth of Phoenix convinced the lawmakers to move it once more. This time the seat of territorial government was housed in more suitable quarters – the new Phoenix city hall. And in 1903 it was moved for the last time – to the newly-constructed capitol building. There, its journeys over at last, it has remained to this day.

Fabulous John Wesley Powell

The young artillery captain lost his right arm, and almost his life, in the Civil War battle of Shiloh, leaving many to believe that thereafter he could see only limited duty.

Some limited duty! John Wesley Powell returned to see action in several more major battles and four years after the war he led one of the most memorable explorations in the history of the West. In 1869 the raging Colorado River, on its course through the Grand Canyon, was almost as uncharted as Mars. No one had ever dared to pilot a boat through its deadly rapids and falls, but Powell was determined to try.

He organized a party of ten men in four wooden row boats to do battle with the Colorado and the Green River which feeds it from Wyoming. A month after their departure from Wyoming on May 24 they had encountered so many perilous rapids that Frank Goodman decided to leave the expedition, telling Powell "I've had enough excitement for a lifetime!"

The party had already lost one boat and most of its supplies, but the most daunting dangers still lay ahead in the heart of the Grand Canyon. Time after time the men faced death, and eventually three more announced their departure. They scaled the cliffs to safety above, only to lose their lives soon thereafter in an attack by Indians. Ironically, only two days after the trio had departed Powell and his five remaining crew reached safety at the mouth of the Virgin River and found settlers placidly fishing from the river bank. Three months had elapsed since the adventurers had departed and they were assumed dead.

Powell's fame has not faded in nearly a century and a half. Lake Powell, on the Arizona-Utah border, is America's second largest man-made reservoir (Lake Mead is the largest) and is one of the nation's most popular recreational treasures.

Conflicts

They didn't call it the "Wild West" for nothing. Like other frontier territories, Arizona attracted hordes of bad guys – men who were wanted by sheriffs elsewhere, and who thought they could get rich in a land of little law enforcement by rustling cattle and robbing stage coaches. Drunken blowhards too often shot it out in rustic saloons, and family feuds took their toll.

Although the Earp-Clanton confrontation near the OK Corral in Tombstone is by far the most famous Arizona gun fight, there were others that brought about more enrichment for territorial undertakers. The feud between the Grahams and Tewksburys, which history calls the Pleasant Valley War, claimed more than thirty lives and a little-remembered unpleasantness in and around St. Johns, which lasted several years, may have filled even more coffins.

But even these were put to shame by the infamous Fort Grant Massacre of 1871, in which a small army of vengeful Tucsonans killed 144 Indians, mostly women and children, who were living outside the fort.

There were conflicts of other sorts – a few duels, military actions, and even a face-off in which Arizona actually declared war on California in 1934 – but Arizona probably had no more of these widely-publicized affairs than other frontier territories. Historian Bert Fireman spent much of his career in trying to demonstrate that most Arizonans were peaceable and most communities never witnessed a gun battle.

However, conflict is more exciting and newsworthy than peaceful living, so the legend of wild and lawless Arizona will likely live on for ages to come.

Arizona Declares War on California

It happened in 1934, but Tempe resident Bob Ricks remembers it like it was yesterday. "I was a buck sergeant in the Arizona National Guard," Ricks recalls, "when Governor (Benjamin) Moeur mobilized us and sent the Guard to the site of the Parker Dam construction on the Colorado River." Moeur's reason: "to repel California's invasion of the sacred soil of Arizona."

He was furious with California's success in gaining high court permission to siphon off untold millions of acre feet of precious Colorado River water, to be captured behind Parker Dam and sent to Los Angeles via a canal. So he declared war on his greedy neighbor and sent the Guard to prevent any attempt to erect dam structures on the Arizona side of the river.

It was no bluff, either. Soon a formidable row of machine guns was lined up, manned by uniformed soldiers and pointed directly at the astonished workmen, who fled in haste. A group of guardsmen borrowed two steamboats from river pilot Nellie Bush and attempted a midnight invasion of "enemy territory." Unfortunately, the boats became entangled with some cables and the embarrassed "Arizona Navy" sailors had to be rescued – by some laughing Californians.

Construction of the dam ground to a standstill while the angry foremen and California politicians struggled to find a solution. They appealed at last to Secretary of the Interior Harold Ickes, who ordered a halt to further construction until some compromise could be worked out with the stubborn Arizona governor. Months passed before Moeur won a concession – authorization of an irrigation project east of Yuma – and Parker Dam moved on to completion.

Chaos in Bisbee!

It was mid-July, 1917. America had entered World War I only a few weeks before, and patriotism beat high in every breast. So it was inevitable that the strike at Bisbee's huge copper mine, fomented by the radical Workers of the World, would be viewed as a crime against the war effort.

In the early morning hours of July 12, some 2,000 vigilantes began rounding up suspected strikers, breaking into homes and dragging them from their beds to a collection point in the city baseball park. Two men were shot and killed in the violent struggles that ensued. Mine officials gave the detainees the chance to be freed if they would swear not to strike, but most refused.

At 11 a.m. a train arrived and 1,186 men were herded onto filthy cattle cars without food, water or a chance to bid their families goodbye. So jam-packed were the cars that none of the deportees could sit down. The heat was almost unbearable and the men were soon crying out in vain for water. Not long after the eastbound train crossed into New Mexico, it stopped in the barren desert and disgorged its human cargo, again without water or food. They were warned not to return to Bisbee if they wanted to go on living.

The strike was broken, but the brutal deportation smeared Arizona's reputation for years to come. Arizona officials took no action against the mine officials or the vigilantes. Some 300 deportees brought civil suits against the copper company and the railroad, but none of the suits ever came to trial. At last one suit against 224 vigilantes came to trial in a state court, but the verdict was predictable: "Not guilty."

A Line of Shame

When the shocking news of Japan's unprovoked attack on Pearl Harbor blared from everybody's radios on that morning of December 7, 1941, Arizonans listened in unbelief and mounting fury. The state's 600-plus loyal Japanese-Americans felt an even more sinister emotion – dread for their future. "What lies ahead for us?" they wondered.

"Segregation? Anti-Japanese laws? Harm from angry neighbors?" What did happen was much worse than they imagined. Leaders of Japanese fraternal and religious organizations were arrested. Bank accounts were frozen. Radios and firearms were confiscated. Curfews were imposed. And finally, an order expelling all Japanese from many areas of the Far West – including all of southern Arizona.

To comply with the exclusion, a line was drawn eastward from Needles, California to Wickenburg, Arizona, thence to the Phoenix area along Grand Avenue, through the heart of Tempe and Mesa, and on to Globe and the New Mexico border. Those Japanese-Americans living south of the line were ordered to move, and 250 were herded into internment camps, fenced and guarded by armed soldiers. They had only a few hours or days to dispose of their farms and other property, receiving an average of ten percent of their actual value. Most Arizona Japanese were sent to the burgeoning camp at Poston on the Colorado River. Some 18,000 Japanese, mostly Californians, went there and another 13,000 were dumped into the Gila River Camp, on the desert near today's Firebird Lake south of Tempe. One can still see some concrete slabs, nails, and other fragments of hastily-erected barracks at the site. There was no air conditioning in the blazing summers and few amenities of any kind.

Almost overnight, the Poston and Gila River camps became the third- and fourth largest "cities" in Arizona. Long after the fear of Japanese infiltration had subsided, the camps were – inexplicably – maintained, and their long-suffering inmates were held captive well into 1945. Six decades later, the shameful incarceration of American citizens is remembered with regret, but the line that once divided Arizona will never be forgotten by those who suffered from it.

Indomitable Frank Luke

Frank Luke's statue stands in a place of honor at the entrance to the Arizona State Capitol in Phoenix. Luke Air Force Base west of Glendale was named for him. He was awarded the Congressional Medal of Honor posthumously. Only the famed Eddie Rickenbacker had more aerial kills during World War I than he, and even Rickenbacker called Luke "the most daring and greatest fighter pilot of the American Air Service." But a relatively few people know that only his death by German gunfire on September 29, 1918 prevented this young Arizonan's arrest and court martial for disobedience of orders.

During the Meuse-Argonne offensive he had been ordered not to fly alone into heavily defended airspace, but he ignored that order and took off in a Spad aircraft to "fight the whole German air force" on his own. It was considered sheer suicide to attack a German observation balloon installation, guarded by a ring of antiaircraft guns and a squadron of fighter planes, but Luke eluded overwhelming enemy fire to shoot down three balloons that day and was headed for a fourth when his luck finally gave out. His plane was disabled and he was wounded by antiaircraft fire, but he managed to land in the midst of a dozen German soldiers. Ignoring orders to surrender, he leaped out and started firing with two pistols. He died from a bullet to his chest, but he left seven dead Germans on the ground. "No one had the sheer contemptuous courage that boy possessed," declared his commanding officer later.

His record of 18 aerial kills is remarkable enough, but there is a postscript that still boggles the mind: Luke scored all those victories during the space of only 17 days!

The Making of a Major General

Baron Goldwater's doctor had warned him that any undue excitement, drinking, or loss of sleep could cause his fragile heart to fail. But on that evening of March 5, 1929 he broke all three rules in presiding over the gala opening of a Goldwater's store in the new Arizona Biltmore and died the next morning of a massive heart attack.

His son Barry immediately interrupted his freshman year at the University of Arizona and came home to train for taking Baron's place as head of the family department store. Barry soon found the retail clothing business too boring and looked around for a new challenge. He found it a few months later when he earned his pilot's license at what became Sky Harbor airport. "My mother didn't like the idea of my risking my hide in a flimsy airplane," he later explained, "so I got up early, before she was awake, to take flying lessons. She said she thought I was having a secret affair, and was a little relieved I told her what I'd been doing."

In early 1941, with American entry into World War II looming, he could not pass the eye exam for pilots, but pleaded unsuccessfully with the commander of the still unfinished Luke Field to let him become an Air Corps flyer. The best the colonel could do was to accept him as a ground officer and a Service Pilot – a designation given civilian airmen. Barry then persuaded several pilots at the base to bend regulations and, on the sly, teach him the Army way to fly. In return, Barry took in-flight photos of his tutors to send home to their girl friends.

Soon he was able to become a full-fledged Air Corps pilot, instructing aerial gunnery at the Yuma Army Air Base. During the war he flew countless missions "over the hump" in the China-Burma-India theater of operations. Upon his return home, he was asked by Governor Sidney P. Osborn to organize and command Arizona's first Air National Guard. That he did, with great success, and remained active in the Air Force Reserve. He flew 165 different military aircraft during his long Air Force service, retiring with the two stars of a major general.

The Mormon Battalion

The Army needed men to fight in the Mexican War and, incidentally, to carve out a wagon road over a southern route to California. Brigham Young had the men, but the new Mormon converts were in the Midwest, without funds to travel to Utah. The easy solution: The Mormons would enlist in the Army and march to southern California, preparing a wagon road as they advanced.

Thus in July of 1846 the Mormon Battalion was born, destined to write an important chapter in Arizona history.

Chosen to command this epic infantry movement was a veteran West Pointer, Lt. Col. Philip St. George Cooke, a cavalry officer who hated this assignment with a passion. He wanted desperately to lead troops into battle in Mexico, and understandably disliked the prospect of herding some 400 untrained rookies across the vast and barren desert. The Mormons soon came to dislike their crusty old commander just as heartily.

But they were stuck with each other, so the battalion left Council Bluffs, Iowa Territory, headed for Santa Fe. They left Santa Fe on October 19, 1846, perhaps more than a little fearful about crossing what was then enemy Mexican territory en route to Tucson and then on to San Diego. Fierce Apaches were even more threatening.

The only combat they encountered on that long march, however, came on November 28, when they encountered a herd of wild bulls near the present site of Benson, Arizona. The ferocious animals charged the advancing troops, goring and killing a number of mules and severely wounding two soldiers before they could be subdued. This "Battle of the Bulls" became an Army legend for decades. The expected battle at Tucson, a Mexican Army stronghold, never materialized. Instead, the Mexicans opted to camp outside the presidio while the Americans rested and replenished their supplies and then moved on to the Gila River and westward to California.

Lt. Col. Cooke came to admire the courage and endurance of his Mormon charges during the tortuous march. In his report he had nothing but praise for them, declaring that "history may be searched in vain for an equal march of infantry. Half of it has been through a wilderness where nothing but savages and wild beasts are found, and across dry deserts where there is no living creature." Cooke hurried to central Mexico in time to see combat action, secure in the knowledge that he had found a southern route to California and cleared the way for wagons to transport the throng of pioneers who soon followed.

Pleasant Valley's Bloody War

On a fateful September morning in 1887 John Tewksbury and William Jacobs stepped outside the Tewksbury cabin in Pleasant Valley and were gunned down by a ring of vengeful members of the Graham clan before they could reach for their weapons. As they lay dying, Tewksbury's frantic wife ran out to aid them, but was forced back inside by another hail of Graham bullets. For several hours the invaders continued to fire into the cabin, from which answering fire kept the Grahams at bay. Meanwhile a drove of wild hogs appeared and started devouring the two lifeless bodies. John's anguished wife grabbed a shovel and, ignoring the deadly fire, ran out to dig shallow graves for the dead men. The Grahams paused while she completed her task, but resumed their attack as soon as she was back in the cabin.

That lurid scene was only one of many enacted in the infamous Pleasant Valley War between the cattle-raising Grahams and the sheep-raising Tewksburys between 1883 and 1892 in the remote valley just below the Mogollon Rim east of Payson. Although little remembered today, it claimed the lives of at least thirty (some say fifty) men – three times the number killed in the more famous Earp-Clanton feud in Tombstone. Its ferocity appalled Arizona Territory citizens and newspaper readers across America. So brutal was the carnage, following hard on Tombstone's OK Corral episode, that it probably delayed Arizona's bid for statehood. Later, Zane Grey glamorized it in his novel *To the Last Man* and Don Dedera published a more reasoned account in his superbly-researched book, *A Little War of Our Own*.

The last standing Graham was shot and killed near the corner of today's Broadway and Priest in Tempe by the last Tewksbury in 1892, but the hatreds kindled by the war burned on for decades. Amazingly, however, not a single participant was ever found guilty of a crime in a court of law.

That Fateful Zimmermann Telegram

© Press Publishing Company

SOME PROMISE! *april 191*

It was March of 1917, when World War I was raging in Europe and President Woodrow Wilson was desperately trying to keep America out of it despite rising public sentiment against the Germans. Every attack on American shipping by German U-boats and horror stories about atrocities against French and Belgian civilians moved us closer to the brink of war. Only a little nudge, it seemed might push us into the bloody conflict.

That fateful nudge came on March 4, when newspapers across the nation headlined the amazing revelation of a message sent to Mexico City by the German foreign minister, Arthur Zimmermann. In it, Zimmermann proposed, among other things, that Mexico should enter the war on the side of the Germans. In return, Germany would see that Arizona and other southwestern territories unjustly grabbed by the U.S. in the Mexican Cession of 1848 would be returned to Mexico.

The message, intercepted and decoded by British cryptographers and rushed to Washington to further inflame American indignation against Germany, caused an immediate uproar in America, and especially in the Southwest. Tucson and Phoenix newspapers wrote blistering anti-German editorials for several days. In a frantic effort to repair the damage, German-language journals in every big eastern U.S. city protested that the message must be a fake dreamed up by British propagandists. But almost immediately, Zimmermann announced to the world that he indeed had sent the telegram and had no regrets about it.

The result was that fateful nudge – likened by some future historians to the later impact of the Japanese attack on Pearl Harbor – that propelled America into the war and sent hosts of young men to fight and die "over there."

50

Tucson Cops Nab Dillinger!

It all started in the pre-dawn of January 21, 1934 when fire engulfed the venerable Congress Hotel in downtown Tucson. Firemen frantically knocked on doors and got all the guests out safely, some in pajamas and others even less covered.

Several of the rescued men persuaded (probably bribed) two of the firefighters to re-enter the hotel and carry their heavy suitcases down from the top floor. When one of the firemen, William Benedict, swore that the man with the biggest bag was a thug whose picture he had seen the day before in *True Detective Mysteries* magazine, police investigated. They identified the thug as Russell Clark, a member of the Dillinger gang and wanted for bank robbery and murder.

His bag, it was later discovered, contained machine guns, ammo and bullet-proof vests. Soon they traced Clark and other gang members to a house in Tucson where they were hiding out with their molls from the nationwide police search.

The police did not arrest them at once, but waited in the hope that John Dillinger himself would soon join the group. Right on schedule, Public Enemy No.1 showed up at the hideout house and walked into a police stakeout. He was arrested without a struggle, and his only comment was "Well, I'll be damned!" A small town police department had succeeded where the nation's top crime fighters had failed.

Dillinger and his pals were brought back to Indiana and imprisoned, but they soon escaped again. Their reign of terror did not end until Dillinger was shot down while leaving a Chicago theater later that year. Eight Tucson police heroes shared $3,300 in reward money, but the two firemen who made it all possible got nothing at all.

Duel to the Death – Sort of

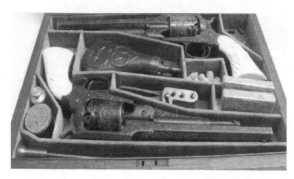

Back in 1859, when Arizona was still the western half of New Mexico Territory, it had only about 3,000 non-Indian residents – a majority of them gamblers, gunmen and fortune-seeking prospectors. Santa Fe, the capital, was a week's horseback ride away and there was little law and order. Phoenix was not yet dreamed of, Tucson was primarily Mexican, and Anglos made up less than half of Tubac's 600 souls.

So it was that a prominent mine owner, Sylvester Mowry, did his best to lure more pioneers to this raw land and started campaigning on behalf of separate territorial status for Arizona. In visits to Washington and other eastern cities he became a one-man chamber of commerce, painting Arizona as a paradise of peace and unlimited potential.

But to Ed Cross, who launched Arizona's first newspaper at Tubac in early 1859, Mowry's efforts were not only dishonest but likely to lure newcomers to their deaths at the hands of murderous Apaches. So Cross condemned Mowry in a series of slanderous editorials. Mowry endured Cross's barrages as long as he could, but at last he challenged his tormenter to a duel to the death, with rifles at some forty paces. Cross accepted, and the two stood back to back one windy Tubac morning and began their march into history.

On the signal to fire, they whirled and fired. But both missed, so they tried again, with the identical result. Finally, after a third miss, Mowry's rifle jammed. Rather than continue the tragicomedy, they shook hands – their honor satisfied – and adjourned with their seconds to celebrate around a large barrel of whiskey.

Politics

Arizona's government got off to an ominous start in 1863 when John Gurley, President Lincoln's choice for governor of the newly-created territory, died before he could start on the long trek to the desert Southwest. So it was that the first governor to serve in Arizona was John Goodwin, a former Maine congressman. He set up shop at Fort Whipple in Chino Valley, but moved the seat of government to the new town of Prescott in the summer of 1864.

You can only imagine the overwhelming problems he and the yet-uncreated legislature faced: trying to count the few scattered citizens of the territory and make those from the South work with those from the North in the midst of the raging Civil War; creating the four original counties (Yavapai, Pima, Mohave and Yuma); setting up judicial machinery; holding elections; establishing governing procedures – all in a land where hostile Indians made staying alive a precarious proposition.

But somehow every obstacle was overcome. The end of the war, and two decades later the elimination of the Indian threat, contributed mightily to the progress of the young territory. Mines flourished, cattle ranches prospered, irrigated farming became profitable, and settlers trickled in to build new towns.

By the time the territorial capital stopped its wandering between Prescott and Tucson and settled down at last in Phoenix (1889), serious efforts to achieve statehood were being launched. As a territory, Arizona faced monumental handicaps. Governors were selected in Washington, legislative actions were subject to Congressional review, and the territory had only one delegate to Congress – and he had no vote. Statehood came at last in 1912, and a 300-pound political wizard from Globe, George Wiley Paul Hunt, began the first of his seven terms as Arizona's state governor. Democrats ruled through most of the early 20th century, and it would not be until the 1950s emergence of Governor Howard Pyle, Senator Barry Goldwater, and Congressman John Rhodes that Republicans had much of a say about the governance of Arizona.

Fremont: Arizona's Worst Governor?

Many of us remember John C. Fremont, "The Pathfinder," whose explorations opened up the American West in the 1840s. He was California's first governor and one of its first two senators – a major general in the Civil War – first presidential nominee of the new Republican Party (he lost to James Buchanan) in 1856 – among other significant achievements. He became a multi-millionaire during the California gold rush, but lost most of his money in failed railway investments. He and his wife Jessie, daughter of famed Missouri senator Thomas Hart Benton, struggled to make ends meet until 1878, when he persuaded his old friend, President Rutherford B. Hayes, to appoint him governor of Arizona Territory, at a meager salary of $2,600 a year.

Apparently, Fremont considered that appointment not as a job but as a reward for past service. Not long after the Fremonts had become settled in Prescott, the territorial capital, he left for New York and Washington to rebuild his fortune and did not return for three months. That was one of his shorter absences. Several other jaunts outside Arizona stretched into six and seven months.

Other territorial officers fretted and complained about his absences, and official business often was left unfinished for long periods. Probably his most memorable action as governor was to launch Arizona's first lottery – a project so poorly managed that it sold only 138 tickets. Meanwhile, the Fremonts lived well beyond their means, forcing Jessie to try her hand at writing for magazines to avoid bankruptcy. She soon proved to be such a skilled writer that her work was published in the best-read journals of that era.

John at last heeded the growing chorus demanding his ouster, and on October 11th, 1881, he submitted his resignation to President Chester A. Arthur.

The Year Arizona Had Two Governors – At Once

Arizona's first state governor, George Wiley Paul Hunt, served seven terms in that office, but getting elected wasn't always easy for him. Although Democrats ruled in the state for most of the early 20th Century, Hunt had antagonized enough of his party leaders to let Republican Tom Campbell win the 1916 governor's race by the ultra-slim margin of 30 votes.

Hunt would not concede, however, so both he and Campbell held separate inauguration ceremonies on January 1, 1917. Hunt, demanding a recount, would not surrender his office in the capitol, so Campbell conducted business at his home. The recount was held, and again Campbell was declared the victor by 30 votes.

Months passed while Hunt sought satisfaction in the Superior Court, with Campbell's pay checks being withheld until the mess could be settled. The court ruled in favor of Campbell, but still Hunt would not surrender. He took his case to the Arizona Supreme Court, where five Democratic justices threw out enough Campbell votes to declare Hunt the winner by 45 votes.

So in December 1917, more than a year after the election, Hunt was undisputed governor at last. Campbell never received a penny for his months of service.

Does this historic fiasco remind you of another election – in Florida – in 2000?

Young Carl Hayden

Carl Hayden
Sheriff of Maricopa County
1909-1912

Those of us who were privileged to know or interview Senator Carl Hayden – revered as "Mr. Arizona" decades before Barry Goldwater earned that title – can hardly picture that ancient, shrunken little man as a youngster. But young he once was, and tall, and a vigorous center on the Stanford University football team.

Even as a child, he was destined for public service, called "my little senator" by his adoring mother. Later he served a record 57 years in Congress and became the most powerful man in the Senate. The only son of Tempe founder Charles Trumbull Hayden, he was born in 1877 in what is now Monti's Casa Vieja on Mill Avenue. He started reading books on history and government even before he was enrolled in the little grade school at the corner of what is now Mill and University.

"I was a mischievous kid," he once told an interviewer. "My mother would have killed me if she had seen me racing down the tops of a line of railroad cars at Tempe's new depot. And she nearly fainted when she learned that I had blown off a finger by pounding on a blasting cap at the flour mill across the street."

Somehow young Carl survived, graduated from the Tempe Normal School in 1896, and enrolled at the recently-established Stanford University. There he played football and could have participated in the first Rose Bowl game (against Michigan) but, as he put it, "it wasn't considered much of a game in those days so I decided to come home for the Christmas vacation."

After graduation, he dabbled in Maricopa County politics and was elected county sheriff. In that post he set a record as the first law man ever to run down a fugitive in an automobile. As Arizona prepared for statehood in the fall of 1911, Hayden decided to run for office as Arizona's lone representative in the House of Representatives and won handily. He went to Washington in February, 1912 and apparently liked it so much that he remained until his retirement from the Senate in 1969 – at age 92.

Thank "Mac" for the G.I. Bill

More than 2.5 million military veterans owe their college education, their home loan and other benefits to one man: Arizona Senator Ernest W. McFarland, hailed as the "Father of the G.I. Bill." A monument at the Arizona state capitol honors him for that hard-won achievement. Remembering his own struggles after Navy service in World War I, he started working for passage of the bill in 1943. President Roosevelt signed it into law a year later.

"Mac," as he was known to many thousands of admirers, was an Oklahoma farm boy, educated in rural schools, before moving to Arizona in 1919 for his health. He earned a law degree at Stanford University and moved up rapidly in Arizona politics – from Pinal County Attorney and Superior Court Judge to the U.S. Senate, where he served from 1941 to 1953 and rose to Majority Leader.

Barry Goldwater defeated him in the 1952 Senate race, scoring an amazing upset, and did so again when McFarland sought to regain his seat in 1958. McFarland was elected Governor of Arizona and later served as Chief Justice of the Arizona Supreme Court. That made him the only person in American history to head all three branches of state government.

With all his achievements, he always had trouble remembering names and faces. Stories abound regarding that shortcoming. Perhaps the best concerns his meeting a constituent at a political rally and saying "I knew your father well. How is he?" "He died six years ago," the man replied. A few moments later he shook hands with the same man and again asked "How is your father?" "Still dead!" came the incredulous response.

George W. P. Hunt: Arizona's Perennial Governor

One man – George Wiley Paul Hunt – held complete domination over the Arizona political scene during the early years of statehood. Not only did he chair the constitutional convention that enabled Arizona to become the 48th state, but he was elected its first governor and was re-elected six times.

Hunt was an almost penniless young man in October, 1881 when he walked into the mining camp of Globe clad in overalls and leading a scrawny burro. The lad was burning with ambition, so much so that he devoted every non-working hour to reading any book he could find and was so successful in the mercantile business that he made a small fortune.

When he turned his attention to Democratic politics, he quickly rose to prominence in the Arizona Legislature. He was a self-taught master of practical politics and won the support of both the working men and many of the corporations that hired them. The more sophisticated populace made fun of his faulty grammar and his coarse manners, but he made political capital out of being a man of the people.

A man of voracious appetites, he ate and drank his way to well over 300 pounds. That massive body and the walrus mustache that he carefully groomed made him an easily recognizable figure wherever he traveled around the new state. But at last his popularity waned, and he was defeated in the 1934 Democratic primary election. That broke the old man's heart, and he died a few months later. He is buried under a white pyramid in Papago Park, near Tempe, a monument visible for miles around.

Raúl Castro Makes Good – REALLY Good

They would call him an illegal alien today and deport him back to Mexico.

Born at Cananea in 1916, Raúl Castro came to the United States at age ten, but did not become a U. S. citizen for several years. Through back-breaking labor and self-denial he made enough money to attend Northern Arizona University, graduating in 1939.

Raúl had a burning desire to be a lawyer and make something of himself. He was graduated from the University of Arizona College of Law in 1949, practiced in Tucson, and in 1954 he launched his political career. First he was elected Pima County Attorney and then a judge on the county Superior Court.

Throughout his climb to political prominence, he was a force in promoting the welfare of his fellow Chicanos. Castro became recognized nationally, and in 1964 President Lyndon B. Johnson appointed him ambassador to El Salvador. He soon gained prominence in Latin America diplomatic circles.

The amazing young Arizona transplant was only beginning to achieve.

Castro returned to Tucson in 1969, practiced international law, and started preparing for a serious bid for a climb in Democratic statewide politics. In 1974 he shocked all the experts by winning his race for Governor on his first try. After two years in the state's highest office, Castro again answered a Presidential call to a major ambassadorship – this time to Argentina by James Carter.

Sadly, the name of Raúl Castro is not well remembered by most of today's Arizonans.

It should not be forgotten.

Our Accidental Governor

Attorney General Bruce Babbitt was sound asleep on that Saturday morning, March 4, 1978 when he was awakened just after sunrise by the insistent jangle of his bedside telephone. "This better be awfully important," he mumbled, "like an earthquake or the end of the world." It was. The message: "You are now Governor of Arizona!"

An attorney general succeeding to the governorship was a 100-to-1 shot, and it culminated a most unusual chain of events. First, Governor Raul Castro left to become U.S. ambassador to Argentina in late October of 1977. That elevated Secretary of State Wesley Bolin, at age 69, to succeed Castro. Bolin had served happily in Arizona's No. 2 position for 28 years and had no ambition to take on the stresses of governing the state. Those stresses probably contributed to the heart attack that killed him four months later, at 3:30 a.m. on March 4, 1978.

Because a secretary of state had not yet been elected, the mantle of leadership passed to Attorney General Babbitt, who at age 39 became the youngest governor in Arizona history. The new governor was not entirely unknown to Arizonans. Grandson of one of the five Babbitt brothers who founded a northern Arizona ranching and commercial dynasty, he had already earned plaudits as one of the best and most energetic attorneys general in Arizona history. He had earned university degrees from Notre Dame, Harvard, and the University of Newcastle in England, and had been active in the Selma, Alabama, civil rights campaign.

Only a few hours after his swearing in as governor, he was on the move, building a reputation for reshaping and vastly strengthening the powers of the governor's office. Arizona voters elected and re-elected him during his nearly nine years as the state's chief executive. Then, on the national scene, he served as Secretary of the Interior and made a spirited run for the Democratic presidential nomination for the presidency.

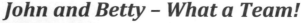

John and Betty – What a Team!

Late in World War II, when Major John Rhodes and his young wife Betty decided to remain in Arizona, they registered to vote. "Republican!" grumbled the surly registrar when they applied. "I don't think my old typewriter will *print* Republican." His shock was understandable, since Arizona at that time had a Democratic superiority of 4 to 1.

But John was adamant, and in 1952 he agreed to run for Congress against firmly entrenched Representative John R. Murdock, who viewed Rhodes' challenge so lightly that he didn't bother to mount a serious re-election campaign. After all, Arizona had never sent a Republican to the U.S. House in all its statehood history. Nobody could have foreseen at that time that John Rhodes would serve for 30 years in Congress and would become a national figure and House Minority Leader.

John's father had been Kansas State Treasurer, and politics was in the younger man's blood. But his wife Betty warned him early in their marriage that only two faults would make her divorce him: adultery and running for office. Once John had determined to run, however, she worked harder than anyone else on his campaign team. At that time, Arizona Congressional District No. 1 comprised all of Maricopa County (District 2 was the rest of the state) so John walked hundreds of miles in blazing heat and rang countless doorbells in his effort to meet voters. There was little money for advertising – only $2,500 in campaign contributions and some $4,000 of his own.

On election day, Congressman Murdock was still a favorite to win. But when the last ballots were tallied around midnight John, with a big boost from the Eisenhower landslide, had pulled off a monumental upset, winning with 53.7 percent of the votes. Next morning, as John and Betty sat at breakfast in their Mesa home, it had just begun to sink in that they were headed for Washington and their lives would never again be the same. "What hath God wrought?" Betty asked in wonderment.

Characters

The West has been blessed with plenty of fascinating characters – those whose personalities and peccadillos set them apart from the common herd – but Arizona seems to have produced more than its share of them. Some, like the Baron of Arizona, gained fame by outrageous thievery. Others, such as Joe Goldwater, seemed always to be coping with a never-vanishing cloud of bad luck. Still others, like Jack Swilling, rose to prominence as a doer of both good and evil. And all of them contributed to the colorful fabric of Arizona history.

We will never forget Dr. Benjamin B. Moeur, whose reputation as a healer of the poor and friendless was exceeded only by his extraordinary mastery of every swear word in the language. Nellie Bush, the "Admiral of the Arizona Navy," and Representative Isabella Greenway and Justice Sandra Day O'Connor powered their way through the barrier of male dominance long before women's liberation became fashionable.

Some Arizona characters were born comics. John Nance gained fame as the most fabled yarn spinner of his day, and Ladd Kwiatkowski had people laughing with his facial gymnastics even before he said a word. Occasionally there was a learned gentleman, like British-born Darrell Duppa, who took off his morning coat and got his hands dirty alongside sweaty miners while earning a star in Arizona history.

There was only one Buckey O'Neill, the fearless lawyer-publisher-sheriff-warrior who led Arizona's contingent of cowboy soldiers in the Spanish-American War. Young Frank Luke, Jr., as brash and untamed a pilot as ever fought battles in the skies, is memorialized by a statue in front of the state capitol. And America will never forget the bravery of Ira Hayes, the Pima Indian Marine who helped raise the flag on Iwo Jima. Or Ernesto Miranda, a youthful Latino whose criminal behavior is less remembered than his role in the landmark Supreme Court ruling that bears his name.

They're all part of the fascinating Arizona legend – ordinary flesh and blood individuals who became extraordinary and will live in our memory for decades to come.

Ladd: Baseball? Comedy?

© WallaceWatchers.com

Ladimir (Ladd) Kwiatkowski was a natural clown if there ever was one. He could contort his rubbery face into amazingly funny expressions, and humor was as natural to him as breathing. But comedy was not his prime passion. Oh, no, that was baseball! As a teenager growing up in Cleveland he worshipped his hometown Indians and vowed to become a professional baseball player himself.

So it was that he decided to take his collegiate studies at the University of Arizona in Tucson, which always has one of the premier baseball programs in America, and which was only a few blocks from the Cleveland Indians spring training home. In the fall of 1949 he scraped together enough money for a bus ticket to Arizona, which was unknown territory to him, and landed in Phoenix. "I wasn't sure where anything was," he once related in an interviewer, "so I asked a stranger where the college campus was. He told me it was about nine miles down the road to the east. I was almost broke, but I took another bus to the next town, Tempe, and was directed to the college, where I enrolled. By the time I discovered I was in the wrong town and at the wrong campus, I was too broke to go any further, so I became a student at Arizona State College, where the baseball coach and players made me feel right at home."

ASC had only a club team at that time, but Ladd and some other recruits started the program on a rapid climb to respectability. Despite the fact that he was clearly the most talented player on the squad, he eventually decided against a baseball career and took a job as a cameraman's assistant at Channel 5 TV in Phoenix. It was not long until he teamed with Bill Thompson and later with Pat McMahon to create the "Wallace and Ladmo Show", a kids' comedy program. Through the next 35 years it reigned as Arizona television's best laugh-provoking series and earned a place in the hearts of millions.

Jack Swilling: Phoenix's Father Was No Model

Jack Swilling (1831-1878) is revered as the Father of Phoenix, but he had a few faults. He was a Confederate Army deserter, barroom brawler, drunk, drug addict, scam artist and two time killer. He died in Yuma County jail at age 47.

But, of course, nobody's perfect.

Born in South Carolina, he fought with Captain Sherod Hunter's Confederate marauders who captured Tucson in 1862. But he soon deserted and later had brief service with the Union Army. Along the way, he took a bullet in his side (it was never removed) and had his skull crushed in a barroom brawl – two misfortunes that left him in constant pain for the rest of his life and led to his morphine addiction.

It was in 1867, after several mining ventures, that he came to the Salt River Valley and discovered the canals that had brought water from the river to a farming community of some 20,000 Hohokam Indians eight centuries before. Excited by this find, he and several friends organized an irrigation company that cleaned the canals and made farming possible here. He started his own farm on the present site of Sky Harbor airport, raised pumpkins and named his new community "Pumpkinville." Fortunately, he and his friend Darrell Duppa changed the name to Phoenix in 1870. He became a family man and upstanding citizen.

Eight years later he was accused (falsely, it was later proved) of robbing a stage coach and was sent to Yuma County jail. There he pleaded for morphine, declaring that he would soon die without it. He was right. A few weeks later he was found dead in his cell.

Amazing Buckey O'Neill

Next time you're in Prescott, take a long look at the famous equestrian statue by Solon Borglum at the north entrance of the downtown plaza. It honors Capt. W. O. (Buckey) O'Neill, one of Arizona Territory's most colorful figures, and his comrades of the Rough Riders in the Spanish-American War.

Buckey crowded more achievements into his 38 years on earth than most of us could claim in three lifetimes. Born in St. Louis in 1860, he became an attorney at age 19 by reading law in Washington, D.C. and came to Arizona in 1879. He set type for Phoenix and Honolulu newspapers, became editor of Prescott's *Arizona Miner*, and was a famed gambler there.

While a court reporter, he was slashed by a knife-wielding madman in a murder trial. Not long thereafter he was elected sheriff of Yavapai County, and later ran successfully for Prescott mayor and then for probate judge. Buckey will always be remembered for the newspaper announcement of his candidacy for judge, declaring that "there are many men more qualified than I, but I need the job!"

Morris Goldwater, Barry's uncle, was Buckey's chief rival on several fronts. Morris was a leading Democrat and Buckey a popular Republican (later Populist). Morris headed one militia company and Buckey another. Morris and Buckey captained rival fire-fighting units and had heated battles in Fourth of July hose company races.

Except for one humiliating incident during a ceremony on the Prescott plaza when, as leader of his militia company, he fainted dead away before a throng of gasping spectators, Buckey was always the admired and dashing hero.

In 1898, O'Neill was the first Arizonan to volunteer for Spanish-American War action with Teddy Roosevelt's Rough Riders. He was appointed captain of Company A and went to Cuba, where he exhibited amazing heroism in leading his men through heavy fire. "The Spanish bullet has never been molded that can hit me!" he declared as enemy rifle fire raked his company. Those were his last words—he was killed a moment later.

All Arizona mourned his passing, and a fund drive was mounted to have his statue erected. The chairman of the drive was none other than his old rival, Morris Goldwater.

Joe Goldwater and the Bisbee Massacre

He was the unluckiest Goldwater of them all. Barry's great-uncle Joe was the only man shot in an Apache raid west of Prescott; the man unjustly jailed and charged with cheating pants-maker Levi Strauss; and the man who narrowly escaped flying bullets in Tombstone's famed Gunfight at the OK Corral. Joe moved south to open a store in the new town of Bisbee, hoping for a more serene life there.

But his dark cloud followed him. On the evening of December 3, 1883, two masked gunmen charged through the door of his store, shouting "hands up!" They ordered Joe to open the safe, but he answered "How can I do that with my hands up?"

"I'll blow your head off if you don't," snarled one robber. Joe complied.

About that time, three other gunmen who had been on guard in front of the store saw a shopper trying to escape from the scene, and shot him dead. It was the first killing in the infamous "Bisbee Massacre." Seconds later a man turned the corner, saw the gunmen, and fled, only to be killed by a second rain of bullets. The third and fourth victims were a woman and her unborn child. The fifth was a man who was fatally wounded as he ran from a saloon.

The bandits eluded a hastily assembled posse, but were soon captured, and all but one sentenced to death by a Tombstone judge. The other, John Heith, was ordered to spend the rest of his life in the Yuma territorial prison. He never got there, however, but was strung up on a pole by enraged citizens. When a photographer appeared, Heith had already been cut down, but the mob obliged him by stringing the corpse up again for a photo that has been printed in scores of Arizona history publications.

John Hance: Arizona's Champion Liar

Visitors to the Grand Canyon in the 1890s looked forward to two memorable experiences: viewing the mighty gorge and meeting John Hance, whose reputation as a spinner of tall tales had spread over much of the West. Hance came to the Canyon about 1885 to prospect for gold, but he found that occupation less profitable than guiding visitors down the steep trails and regaling them with his stories around campfires at night.

One of his favorite tales was about the time he and his pet mule, Darby, encountered a dense fog over the gorge. "We couldn't see our way," he declared, "so we waited until night when the temperature dropped and froze that fog so solid that we rode clear across to the north rim!"

Another time, he recalled, he and Darby were pursued by bloodthirsty Indians until they reached the canyon rim. "There was only one way to save my life," he swore, "and that was to jump across. We got a good running start and sailed out into space, but soon we were hurtling down, down to the river below. It looked like the end for me, but I remembered that Darby always obeyed my commands. So I shouted 'whoa!' and that mule came to a dead stop not three feet above the canyon floor!"

His whoppers sometimes got Hance into serious trouble, however. "One day a stranger asked me how the deer hunting was around the south rim," he told a crowd around an evening campfire. "I told him it was real good, and that I had killed three deer myself that morning. Then he asked if I knew who he was, and I said 'no.' 'I'm the game warden,' he told me. I was flabbergasted. 'Do you know who I am?' I shot back. He said 'no.' 'Well,' I said, 'I'm the biggest damn liar for miles around!'"

The Baron of Arizona

James Addison Reavis, a one-time St. Louis streetcar motor-man, hit Tucson like a bomb in 1882 and declared that he owned a strip of central Arizona land 235 miles wide and 75 miles deep, including Phoenix and everything east to New Mexico and beyond. What's more, he had ancient Spanish land grant documents to back up his claim. The United States had agreed in the Treaty of Guadalupe Hidalgo (which ended the Mexican War) to honor all Spanish land grants if they could be legally documented.

Reavis produced what he said were the centuries-old Peralta Grant papers, which he had painstakingly forged over several years of preparation in Madrid and Mexico City for his outrageous con game. In addition, he had documents showing him to be a descendant of the Peralta family. He then threatened to evict every home owner and commercial business from his land. So convincing was Reavis that the Southern Pacific Railroad, ranch owners, and private residents grudgingly paid him handsome sums for quit claim deeds to clear their land titles – some half a million dollars in all. For several years, Reavis lived like a king with his ill-gotten gains, earning him the title of "The Baron of Arizona."

But his victims hired experts in an effort to prove that the documents were forgeries. At last they found that the lettering on the papers was of fairly recent design and written with pen and ink not yet in use when the Peralta grant was made by the Spanish king. The "baron" was tried in federal court in 1895 and was found guilty. But he conned the judge into letting him off with only a two-year sentence and a $5,000 fine. Reavis died penniless in 1914.

The Lord Who Named Us

"Lord" Darrell Duppa was as colorful a character as any who roamed the vast Arizona Territory in the mid-19th Century – a learned English aristocrat who claimed the title "Lord" but lived more like an impecunious peasant – a man whom a friend described as a hermit who "would go off in the mountains and stay until his hair reached his shoulders, hardly looking like a human." An inveterate gambler, he usually blew his substantial remittances from home not long after they arrived.

But Duppa was much more than a harmless eccentric. Born in France (his father was a British diplomat), he spoke five languages, was a student of the classics, traveled all over Europe, engaged in the wool business in New Zealand, and came to Arizona in 1863 after prospecting for gold in California. Here he was wounded in each of three battles with Apaches, but stayed on, he said, "to show them I could!"

In Prescott, where he lived and prospected for four years, he was regarded with awe by the semi-literate miners who were much impressed by his learning. Duppa was one of the first to settle in the Salt River Valley. Among his friends was canal builder Jack Swilling, revered as the "Father of Phoenix." Swilling wanted to call the new village Pumpkinville, and others suggested Salina. But Duppa, reminding them that the settlement was rising on the remains of the ancient Ho-ho-kam community, urged that it be called Phoenix, after the mythical bird which rose from its own ashes. His neighbors agreed.

Later, when the new town across the Salt River was known as Hayden's Ferry, Duppa said the area reminded him of the Vale of Tempe, in Greece. So Tempe it became, and even founder Charles Trumbull Hayden agreed that "at least the new name will save ink."

You Didn't Know He Was an Arizonan?

The little Italian-American kid was an Army brat, son of the Bandmaster at Fort Whipple near Prescott. He arrived in Arizona Territory in 1890 with his parents and half a dozen siblings and was enrolled in the fourth grade at the Prescott elementary school. It was natural for him to love music and to play the cornet in his family orchestra, but the other boys in his school – whose idols were rugged frontier cowboys – often teased him because of his small size (he never grew taller than 5'-2") and lack of athletic ability. But the shy youngster shook off their taunts and dreamed of a career in some field of music.

At his elementary school graduation, when his classmates recited poems or bits of Shakespeare, he chose to play a cornet solo instead. He was 16 when the family left Prescott, and by that time he had decided on a career in law in New York City, where he was born. No longer shy, he impressed Republican leaders in his borough, who urged him to enter the political arena. Eventually his engaging personality led him to a successful run for mayor of America's largest city, and he served three terms during the Depression years.

Both friends and foes nick-named him "Little Flower," a play on his short stature and his Italian first name, and he is still remembered for such kindnesses as that of reading the comics over the radio to children when New York newspapers were on strike. Few mayors of the Big Apple were more popular. He never forgot his Arizona roots, however, and in 1938 he returned to Prescott as a guest of famed historian Sharlot Hall and was feted as a local hero. His name is remembered in Prescott with the naming of a bridge on Sheldon Street: Fiorello LaGuardia Bridge.

Lillico: Sometimes He Broke the Rules

From the moment when he fell into an open man hole while turning to wave his ever-present cigar at a friend, flamboyant Tom Lillico was known as "Blind Tom." The first sports recruiter ever hired by Arizona State Teachers College at Tempe (now ASU), he turned the lackluster Bulldog football program around and assembled a razzle-dazzle team that went to the Sun Bowl in 1940 and 1941. Tom was never one to abide strictly by the rules, either written or unwritten. He brought the first Black player to Tempe in 1937 – ignoring the tacit law of the Border Conference against such effrontery – and soon thereafter he snatched three prize recruits from the grasp of rival University of Arizona (the UA was so irked by that piracy that they refused to play ASTC for the next four years).

Most of his recruiting triumphs were legal, but he did stray on occasion – like the time he brought Jep Shamblee to play for Tempe. The fact that Jep had played for Alabama along with Dixie Howell in the 1935 Rose Bowl game and was strictly ineligible didn't bother him a great deal. And old Bulldog fans recall with glee how Tom rushed to the timer's table in a basketball game against New Mexico at Albuquerque and fired a gun ending the game. Nobody complained much, because the home-town timer had been trying to extend the game until New Mexico got the lead.

When Dixie Howell came to coach the Tempe football team in 1938, he and Tom became close friends. Howell was a national hero in his day, but he was shy about speaking in public and turned down invitations to address Arizona high school sports banquets. One evening Lillico tricked him into attending Chandler High School's football banquet, and informed him after they arrived that he was to be the featured speaker. Dixie was flabbergasted, but he had no choice but to mount the podium. Once there, talking about football, he found himself enjoying the limelight. Basking in the glow of adoring fans after the dinner he grabbed Tom and asked "Where do you want me to speak next?" It was the start of a new career for Dixie, who later made his living in public relations.

Elliott Roosevelt: Arizonan

He was called the black sheep of Franklin Roosevelt's children – famous around the world for his scandalous behavior, his five marriages, his book revealing his father's amours with Lucy Mercer and Missy LeHand, and much more. He knew the leaders of a dozen countries and hob-nobbed with celebrities from Hollywood to Broadway.

Most American knew about him, but few were aware that Elliott was at heart an Arizonan. His first job was as manager of a small airline owned by Isabella Greenway in Tucson. Before that he was a bull rider on the rodeo circuit. His third wedding (to actress Faye Emerson with Howard Hughes as best man) was at the Grand Canyon. He owned three homes in the Phoenix area and spent his final years with his fifth wife in Scottsdale. It was in Scottsdale, in 1990 at age 80, that he died.

Among his many headlined adventures was his arrest on a charge of drunken driving in front of his favorite bar, Scottsdale's Pink Pony. Another was his unsuccessful battle to become a member of the Paradise Valley Country Club, whose Roosevelt-hating officers black-balled him. When Barry and Bob Goldwater learned of his plight, they sponsored him for membership in the Phoenix Country Club.

Elliott met his last wife in a typically bizarre way. Patty Peabody Whitehead, then a real estate agent, came to his Phoenix home to help him sell it and was touring the master bedroom when Elliott burst from the shower stark naked and shouted "get the hell out of here!" Later, when he was dressed and Patty had recovered from shock, he was his suave and gentlemanly self, and the two started their romance not long thereafter. Patty had much to do with taming the former playboy during their happy marriage. Amazingly, he converted to the Catholic Church and became a regular attender. He joined the Rotary Club, took part in civic affairs and charitable endeavors, and gained new fame for writing his series of murder mysteries starring his mother as the protagonist. Moreover, the one-time womanizer was the most faithful of husbands. He and Patty celebrated their thirtieth anniversary not long before he died.

Ma! That Man Killed Santa Claus!

It was Christmas season, but business in downtown Mesa stores was crawling to a near halt in that Depression December of 1932. Merchants were frantic as they tried to conjure up some kind of exciting event that would bring in crowds and start the cash registers ringing again. Then came John McPhee to the rescue. McPhee, the bright young editor of the city's weekly newspaper, the *Mesa Journal-Tribune*, came up with a truly novel idea: Instead of something mundane, such as bringing in Santa on the decorated flatbed of a truck, why not fly him in aboard an airplane and have him parachute down to the cheering mob below?

In those early days of aviation, people were still excited to see an airplane pass overhead. Surely, the chance to see Santa float down from a plane would attract thrill-starved residents (all potential shoppers) to Mesa by the hundreds.

For years to come Charlie Mitten, long-time publisher of the newspaper, told and re-told the story of McPhee's memorable day in the limelight. The editor arranged for a plane and pilot, and convinced a reluctant Santa to make the death-defying leap. Unfortunately, however, the jolly old elf tried to prop up his courage with moonshine whiskey and arrived at the scene too drunk to perform.

McPhee was not ready to disappoint the crowd, however, so he tore off the man's Santa suit, stuffed and weighted it, hooked on the parachute, and signaled the pilot to take off. Moments later the plane appeared above the throng and Santa came tumbling out. But the parachute failed to open and Mr. Claus came crashing to earth as the crowd gasped in dismay. Women fainted, children wailed, and their wrathful parents went looking for McPhee. He somehow survived, but throughout his newspaper career he could never shake the title of "The Man Who Killed Santa Claus".

Tom Mix's Last Ride

His name was Thomas Hezikiah Mix, better known as "Tom Mix, King of the Cowboys," and in the 1920s and 1930s he was more famous than Presidents Coolidge or Hoover. Most kids, in America and around the world, worshipped him and rarely missed a Saturday afternoon movie or serial episode that starred their hero. Tom loved Arizona, lived here part time, and competed in many rodeos around the state. Prescott's Frontier Days show was a special favorite of his, and he delighted in showing off his many cowboy skills in the Mile High City.

Although better known for his flashy attire and extravagant lifestyle, he could handle a horse, a lariat, and a pistol with the best of them. Tom gloried in driving fast cars, pursuing beautiful women (he married five of them), and holding court at bars all over the West. At 18, in 1898, he enlisted in the Army during the Spanish-American War, but didn't see action in Cuba. Instead, he departed his unit without leave and never bothered to return. But that didn't stop his movie publicists from claiming in later years that he fought with Teddy Roosevelt's Rough Riders. After his first movie role in 1910 he starred in more than 300 films, all but nine of them silents.

He earned an amazing six million dollars, but spent most of it during his riotous life. On the rainy late afternoon of October 12, 1940, after a number of drinks at the Santa Rita Hotel in Tucson, he climbed into his souped-up Cord Phaeton and roared off toward Prescott. Near Florence, on a stretch of dirt road, he came upon a flooded arroyo and failed to see workmen attempting to repair the bridge. At a speed estimated at 75 miles per hour, he plowed into the ravine, sending a metal suitcase behind him slamming against the back of his head and breaking his neck. The King of the Cowboys died instantly. The nation mourned his untimely death, and a metal marker in the shape of a riderless horse was erected on the spot. Visitors still come and pay homage to his memory at what has been named "Tom Mix Wash" on State Highway 79.

Will Rogers Made Them Laugh

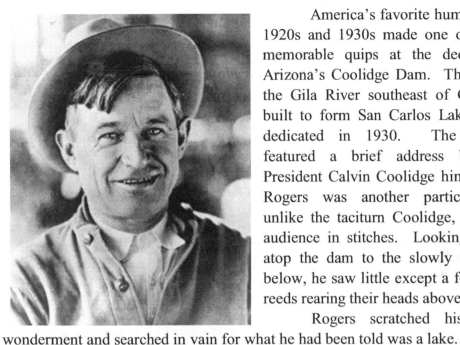

America's favorite humorist of the 1920s and 1930s made one of his most memorable quips at the dedication of Arizona's Coolidge Dam. That dam, on the Gila River southeast of Globe, was built to form San Carlos Lake and was dedicated in 1930. The ceremony featured a brief address by former President Calvin Coolidge himself. Will Rogers was another participant and, unlike the taciturn Coolidge, he had his audience in stitches. Looking out from atop the dam to the slowly filling lake below, he saw little except a forest of tall reeds rearing their heads above the marsh.

Rogers scratched his head in wonderment and searched in vain for what he had been told was a lake.

"If that was MY lake," he declared, "I'd mow it!"

Then Rogers turned his humor onto Coolidge. Old timers who were present recalled the quips he aimed at the stodgy New Englander.

"There's old Cal," he mused. "Times were pretty good when he was in the White House. He never said much, which we appreciated. (laughter). And he didn't do much, either. But that was just what we wanted him to do! (roaring laughter)."

Coolidge was not amused. The *Arizona Republic's* Reg Manning, who was seated near the podium, declared that Coolidge never cracked a smile.

Dr. Chandler Knew They Would Come

People were sure that Dr. Alexander J. Chandler had lost his mind in 1911 when he talked of building a fantastic luxury hotel and resort on the barren stretch of desert south of Mesa. Dr. Chandler, a Canadian who came to Arizona in 1891 as the first Territorial Veterinarian, created a town site on the property (named for him) and began making his dream come true.

He was a dreamer of long standing, having left his veterinary practice before the turn of the century and made a fortune in canal building, land development, and half a dozen other enterprises. His Chandler Ranch covered 18,000 acres. At one time he built an electrical generating complex that supplied power to residents of Tempe and other nearby towns.

But a luxury resort? On the desert, half a day's drive from Phoenix?

Impossible! Dr. Chandler listened to all the reasons why his latest dream was sheer madness and charged ahead, aided by his friend Frank Lloyd Wright. On November 22, 1913, the San Marcos Hotel and Resort, named for Marcos de Niza, the priest who was the first white man to enter Arizona, played host to a grand opening crowd of 500, including Vice President Thomas Marshall, Governor George W.P. Hunt, Congressman Carl Hayden, several movie headliners, and the cream of Arizona society.

Eventually the guest list included Gloria Swanson, Bing Crosby, Herbert Hoover, Christian Dior, and a host of other celebrities. The San Marcos was the first Arizona resort to offer polo, as well as horseback riding, golf, tennis, swimming and famed cuisine. Its ballroom was the scene of many an eye-popping formal dance. "If you build it they will come," was a motto Dr. Chandler believed in. So he did, and they did. His dream came true and his hotel is still one of Arizona's finest.

Women

Only during the past few decades have many women played major roles in the development of Arizona. The iron hand of male dominance, which for the most part kept them on the sidelines, and even without the right to vote, imprisoned Arizona women "in their place." But look at them now! We now have had female mayors and judges and Congressional representatives; governors, and even a Supreme Court justice.

Governor Janet Napolitano was chosen by President Obama to serve in his cabinet as Secretary of Homeland Security. She was succeeded as governor by Secretary of State Jan Brewer. For two years early in this 21st century, women held all five of the top elective offices in the state.

To read the Arizona history books, one might assume that few women made much of an impact during our formative years. But there have been many who helped shape the Arizona of today. Martha Summerhayes, for example. She came as the bride of a young officer not long after the end of the Civil War, endured the hardships of a slow steamboat ride up the Colorado in the heat of summer and the dangers of life in remote Army posts during the Indian wars, and wrote a book about those years. That book, *Vanished Arizona*, is still treasured as the best account of frontier existence we have today. Long before Martha's coming, Sarah Bowman trekked across the desert during the Mexican War and earned the title of "First Citizen of Yuma."

Sharlot Hall will always be honored for her decades of labor in preserving pioneer documents and memorabilia that otherwise would have been lost. Nellie Bush, "Admiral of the Arizona Navy," helped lay the foundations of several Colorado River communities and later was the second woman to be elected to the Arizona Legislature. Isabella Greenway was an entrepreneur of rare talent who served in Congress after establishing herself as a leader in southern Arizona business and politics.

The list goes on, climaxed by the name of Sandra Day O'Connor, the ranch girl who earned a Stanford law degree and became the first woman to serve on the U.S. Supreme Court.

Just as vital to the development of Arizona as these outstanding ladies are the host of unsung wives and mothers who bolstered their husbands and nurtured the children who grew up to provide leadership in so many fields of endeavor.

We salute them all!

A Brave Lady Transforms Phoenix

Her twisted little body was a bundle of unending arthritic pain, so she had every excuse to give up and take to her bed. But Mrs. Archer E. Linde refused to take the easy way out. Because of her undaunted courage, Phoenix got its first real taste of the performing arts in the 1930s and started up the long road to cultural excellence.

Born Jeanette Harper at Streator, Ill. in 1887, she sang with the St. Louis Opera Company for a time. She married Mr. Linde and in 1920 moved with him to Phoenix for her health. Appalled by the virtual non-existence of first class music and drama here, she vowed to bring national stars to the desert. By 1930 she had made important contacts with performers and agents, and in 1936 she opened her one-woman business, Linde Box Office Productions.

But where could the stars of stage and concert halls perform if they came? Mrs. Linde worked her magic, persuading Vladimir Horowitz to perform in the Phoenix Union High School gymnasium. Even more magical was her success in bringing the Ballet Russe to dance in the school's little auditorium. The biggest names in the entertainment business – Charles Laughton, Ezio Pinza, Mario Lanza, Liberace, major symphony orchestras, and scores of other headliners – were among the stars of the 750 events she lured to Phoenix.

She brought Marian Anderson, Paul Robeson and many other African-American stars to Phoenix, and put them up in her own home because hotels refused to accept them. When some white patrons complained about being seated next to those of dark skins, she answered, "If you don't like it, don't come!" At every performance she urged the audience to support construction of a suitable theater and concert hall. Mrs. Linde died in 1965, seven years before the opening of Phoenix Symphony Hall, but the memory of this remarkable cultural advocate will live on for many decades to come.

Isabella Greenway: What a Woman!

Isabella Ferguson had fallen wildly in love. But, unfortunately, the object of her affection was not her husband, Robert, 18 years her senior. Her new love was handsome, dashing John Greenway, one of Arizona's most prominent copper barons and founder of the town of Ajo.

For several years they kept their romance chaste and secret, but one day in 1913 John felt it his duty to tell Ferguson that he and Isabella were in love. Greenway offered to leave the country, but he agreed to a lesser sentence: his promise that he and Isabella would never be alone together as long as Ferguson lived. John kept that promise, but within a few months after Ferguson's death in 1922 he and Isabella were married.

John's responsibilities at copper mines in southern Arizona and Mexico kept him away from Isabella for weeks at a time, during which she began to demonstrate the rare abilities that were to make her one of Arizona's most famous women. She already had exhibited her talent as a ranch manager in New Mexico, and now she plunged into Democratic politics, managing a furniture manufacturing business, buying and managing a ranch near Williams in northern Arizona, launching a small airline, and eventually being elected to the U.S. House of Representatives – the first Arizona woman to serve in Congress.

But she is perhaps best remembered today for creating and managing the Arizona Inn in Tucson, still one of the state's premier resort hotels. Through all this flurry of activity she nourished her life-long friendship with Eleanor Roosevelt. Isabella and Eleanor had been New York City debutantes, and Eleanor chose her as a bridesmaid at her wedding to future president FDR.

Isabella's love story has a tragic ending: John Greenway, who had waited for 13 years to marry her, sickened and died only two years after they were wed.

Nobody Quite Like Jo

Her ticket to Phoenix was not at the Ash Fork depot as promised, so spunky little Hattie Josephine Williams started walking south along the tracks. Moments later a freight train lumbered by and a friendly brakeman scooped her up and deposited her in the caboose, just behind a fragrant cattle car. That's how the tiny nurse from Nebraska made her entrance into Phoenix in October, 1903. Not in her wildest dreams could she have imagined that she was destined to become one of Arizona's most celebrated women.

Jo, as most people called her, had tuberculosis, and Chicago doctors gave her only six months to live. But she was not one to give in. Living in a tent on the desert north of Phoenix, she baked in the sun for many months while nursing other "lungers." Then in 1906, with a clean bill of health, she moved into town and shopped for some clothes suitable for city wear. In Goldwater's department store, she was waited on by the owner himself: Baron Goldwater, acknowledged by everyone as the most eligible bachelor in Phoenix. Baron was captivated by her, and on New Year's Day, 1907, they were married in St. Luke's Episcopal Church, Prescott. Their choice of churches was a compromise, since Baron was Jewish and Jo Presbyterian.

Their first child, whom they named Barry Morris Goldwater, was born on New Year's Day of 1909. Bob arrived in 1910, and Carolyn in 1912. Jo gave them all free rein: romped and camped and hunted and golfed with them. The Goldwater home became such a rowdy mad house that fastidious Baron ate most of his evening meals at the Arizona Club.

Jo was a free spirit who cared little what her friends in Phoenix high society thought about her. She wore trousers, drank a bit too much, and was one of the first women in town who smoked. She could swear like a mule skinner when irritated. Jo loved the outdoors, was a crack shot with a rifle, and was twice state women's golf champion.

Above all, she was a friend of underprivileged and unfortunate people, who never forgot her kindnesses. Everyone who knew her came to respect and love her – none more so than her adoring children. Her husband died of a heart attack in 1929, but the young nurse who came to Phoenix to die lived until she was 91.

The Oatman Family Massacre

Everyone in Tucson in December, 1850 warned Royce Oatman not to venture with his wife and six children across the Indian-infested desert 230 miles to Fort Yuma on the Colorado River. But they had been traveling for months from Independence, Missouri, and he was in a hurry to get to the promised land called California. At the Pima Villages (not far south of today's Gilbert), they hoped to buy food from the friendly Indians, but the natives had none to sell. So, with scant provisions and no protection, they started west along the present Interstate-8 route.

On the evening of February 18, 1851, some thirty miles west of Gila Bend, the family made camp and prepared to eat their last bread crusts and bean soup. Suddenly a band of hostile Yavapai Indians appeared and demanded food. When they found there was none, they started beating the terrified Oatmans with clubs until both parents and four children lay dying on the ground. They took two screaming girls, 14-year old Olive and 10-year old Mary Ann, as slaves, but a teen-aged son, Lorenzo, later regained consciousness and survived.

"They made us run barefoot across the stony ground to their camp, many miles away," recalled Olive years later. "My feet were cut and bleeding. I couldn't stop crying and I prayed to die along with my family."

Both girls were given hard labor to do, and were beaten repeatedly. Mary Ann died from abuse and starvation after a year of captivity. Olive was sold to a Mohave chief, who tattooed her chin with black stripes to show she was now a tribal member.

Five years passed, but Olive's brother never gave up searching for her. Then one day there came a report of a white woman living with the Mohaves. An Indian messenger volunteered to try to buy her freedom, offering a horse, a blanket and some trinkets. It was enough. She was brought back for a tearful reunion with Lorenzo, and newspapers all over the country trumpeted the amazing story. Olive had become more Indian than white, but after a few months she was able to resume her place in the white world. She soon married and lived in Texas until her death at age 66.

How We Almost Lost Tempe

For one breathless moment in late 1876, Tempe's future hung by a thread as an unhappy woman tried to make up her mind. The woman was Sallie Davis Hayden, only recently married to Charles Trumbull Hayden, founder of the city, which was named Hayden's Ferry at that time.

Hayden had settled at the foot of what we now call "A Mountain" in 1871, built an adobe house (now Monti's Casa Vieja), opened a ferry service across the Salt River, began operating a flour mill, and launched half a dozen other businesses along Mill Avenue.

In 1876, when he was 51, he decided the time had come for him to marry. So he went to Visalia, California, where he had met a 35-year old school teacher, Sallie Davis, and proposed. She hardly knew Hayden, but she realized she had better marry soon if she wanted to have a family. So they wed.

When she reached Hayden's Ferry, after a bone-shaking ride in Hayden's freight wagon, the starkly barren appearance of the place shocked her. "My heart fell clear to my shoes!" she later told her daughter Sallie. Hayden left on a business trip a few days after their arrival, leaving her to cope with heat, loneliness, a house with dirt floors, and scantily clad Indians peering at her through dingy windows. She was determined to put up with it all, and did so for several months.

But at last Hayden became aware of her overwhelming unhappiness. "He sat down with me," she recalled later, "and made a startling proposal. He said 'All I have is here, my dear, but if you cannot be happy in this place, we will move anywhere you wish to go and I will start over.' For a moment I wanted to shout yes, yes! but I didn't. I realized what a great sacrifice he was willing to make for my sake, so I gritted my teeth and said I would stay." A month later, she discovered she was pregnant. Her cares were swept aside as she prepared for the birth of her first child, Carl, who was destined to become the most famous Arizonan of his era and the most powerful man in the U.S. Senate.

Soiled Doves and Shady Ladies

Old time Arizonans used to swear that if a prospector struck gold in the morning, practitioners of the world's oldest profession would be on the scene by sundown. First in tents, then in shacks, and later in ornate pleasure palaces, they came in droves to the territory's mining camps and cattle towns. Lonely miners and cowboys welcomed them with open arms and open pockets. There was a time when ladies of the evening made up a sizeable portion of the female population of Arizona, and they played a more important role in civilizing the rough frontier than most people are aware.

They imported the first pianos, the fanciest furniture, the latest fashions, and the finest wines. In the better houses, patrons were denied admission unless they were clean and behaved like gentlemen. More important, many of the ladies nursed the sick and collected money for down-and-outers. They were not all angels of mercy – far from it. Most were as tough as boot leather and the worst of them were notorious thieves, cheats, and barroom brawlers.

Among the more memorable good girls was China Mary, who nursed many a sick or injured man back to health in her home and never asked for any payment. Eventually she returned to China, married, and lived respectably ever after. Irish Mag often fell for a prospector's plea for grubstake money. One lucky miner struck pay dirt and shared his good fortune with her. She immediately took the money and returned to her native Ireland. Miss Jenny, whose house burned down in two Jerome fires, is said to have offered volunteer firemen free service if they would come to her establishment first if fire broke out again. They happily accepted, and left other buildings to blaze away.

One of the best known of these frontier entrepreneurs was Big Nose Kate, who was Doc Holliday's live-in girl friend in Tombstone. In an era when most soiled doves died young of disease or violence, she operated businesses in several Arizona towns and retired to the Arizona Pioneers Home in Prescott, where she died five days short of her 90th birthday.

Winnie Ruth Judd: Trunk Murderess?

On that late October day in 1931 the baggage master at Los Angeles Union Station suspected it was blood oozing from the steamer trunk just arrived from Phoenix. He was right. Upon opening the lid, he saw something that nearly caused him to faint: a young woman's body crammed inside, her knees under her chin. A smaller trunk nearby bore even more gruesome contents: a woman's torso, cut at the navel. Her three remaining body parts, stuffed into bags, were later found in a nearby ladies' room.

The 26-year-old physician's assistant – Winnie Ruth Judd – who shipped the trunks to Los Angeles had hoped, with a brother's help, to dump them into the ocean. But the seeping blood spoiled her plan. Within the hour, newspaper headlines all across America were shouting out the story of a murder that still ranks among the most bizarre in the nation's history.

The two victims had been Winnie Ruth's best friends, Anne LeRoi and Hedvig Samuelson. On the night of October 16, 1931, the three somehow got into a screaming brawl at a midtown Phoenix home and Winnie Ruth, according to a later interview, wrested a loaded pistol from Hedvig "to defend myself" and killed both of the others with shots to the head.

In near-shock, she telephoned her secret lover, a married man who was in the top level of Phoenix society, and hysterically asked what she should do. Anxious to keep a lid on the scandal and protect his good name, he promised he would "take care of everything." What he allegedly did was to persuade a doctor friend to cut up the bodies and put them in trunks to be shipped by rail to Los Angeles. But the newspapers shouted that Winnie Ruth had been the butcher and painted her as the most fiendish of criminals.

Such was the climate when her trial opened in Phoenix on January 19, 1932. It was to be perhaps the most sensational and most widely reported trial in Arizona history.

Winnie Ruth's trial in the new Phoenix courthouse was a disgraceful sham. She never had a chance. The nation's newspapers, led by William Randolph Hearst's 33 scandal sheets, painted her as a demonic monster before any evidence was presented. Both the *Arizona Republic* and *Phoenix Gazette* joined the "guilty" chorus and would not print findings to the contrary. Her lover would not lift a finger on her behalf. Her lawyer refused to mention the possibility of self defense during the trial and would not even permit her to testify in her own behalf. The defense based its case entirely on the presumption of insanity.

Winnie Ruth, a pretty and petite figure of less than 110 pounds, sat almost expressionless during the nightmarish proceeding, twisting a lace handkerchief to shreds.

The jury deliberated only four hours and its verdict was inevitable: Guilty of murder in the first degree, and death by hanging. But the powers that be did not want to hang a woman. Instead, an insanity hearing was hastily scheduled and Winnie Ruth was committed to the Arizona State Hospital. There she remained, except for a half-dozen highly publicized escapes, for the next 39 years. In 1971, Governor Jack Williams at last pardoned her.

It was not until noted Phoenix journalist Jana Bommersbach launched her personal crusade on Winnie Ruth's behalf and wrote her sensational 1992 book, *The Trunk Murderess: Winnie Ruth Judd,* based in part on the only interview Winnie ever gave a writer, that the full truth of the case was revealed.

Bommersbach's conclusions: "They said she was a cold-blooded killer. They said she hacked up her best friend. They said she was insane. They said she acted alone. Yet to this day the questions remain about just how guilty Winnie Ruth Judd was."

The Admiral Was a Lady

Nellie Bush, who was born in 1888, pre-dated the Women's Liberation movement, but you can be sure she would have been a leader of it. She was a lawyer, state legislator, justice of the peace, airplane pilot, school principal, business woman, and coroner. But she is best remembered for her feats as a Colorado River steamboat pilot and the only person honored by an Arizona governor as "Admiral of the Arizona Navy."

Nellie's boldness in breaking the "men only" customs of so many occupations was first noted when she dared to enroll in the University of Arizona law school in 1921. There she challenged the rule that females could not be present when such delicate subjects as rape were being discussed. "Did you ever hear of a rape case that did not involve a woman?" she asked the professor. He had to admit that she had a point, and let her participate in the discussion.

She and her husband moved to Parker in 1915 and bought the ferry boat business there. In 1934 Nellie and her two steamboats participated in the ill-fated "war" which Governor Benjamin Moeur launched against California in an effort to halt construction of the Parker Dam. In gratitude for her service, Moeur honored her with the title "Admiral of the Arizona Navy."

Self-sufficient in every way, she once was stranded in the desert east of Parker when her car suddenly ground to a halt. Lifting the hood, she replaced a broken spring with a hair pin and went merrily on her way. Her only known failures were in her runs for Congress in the 1930s, and even then she lost by surprisingly narrow margins. Nellie Bush died at age 75 in 1963, and later was one of the first honorees in the Arizona Women's Hall of Fame.

Yuma's First Citizen – The "Great Western"

The biggest passenger ship to sail the ocean in 1850 was affectionately called the "Great Western," so it seemed appropriate to slap that nickname on Sarah Bowman. After all, she stood 6 feet, 2 inches tall, weighed nearly 200 pounds, and could (and sometimes did) lick any man in one of the western taverns she frequented.

Sarah was a red haired, blue eyed giant whose fame as a fearless fighter first bloomed during the Mexican War, when she braved enemy fire to bring water to thirsty troops and fire a gun if that became necessary. But she is best remembered as the first citizen of Arizona City, the Colorado River town later renamed Yuma. She made a good living running a boarding house in the town, offering good food and more unmentionable services to lonely soldiers at Fort Yuma. Her adobe boarding house became a bordello and she was able to hire some of the most attractive women in nearby Mexico.

What endeared her most to the Fort Yuma troops was her willingness to nurse sick and wounded soldiers back to health, and to be a friend to anyone who needed one. Author Raphael Pumpelly visited Yuma in 1861 and noted that Sarah was the only permanent resident of the town. When Fort Yuma was evacuated during the early days of the Civil War she closed up shop, sent her ladies back to Mexico, and followed the Union's California Column in its march through Arizona in 1862. Sarah was a loyal servant to the Army almost until her death in 1866 at age 54. So exemplary were her services to the Union troops that the War Department directed that her remains be carried in honor from Fort Yuma and reburied at the Presidio in San Francisco.

Sharlot Hall: She Rescued Our History

The tough little lady from Kansas scoffed at the widely-held notion that women should be kept barefoot and pregnant – out of leadership roles and devoted only to keeping the home fires burning. Sharlot Hall was only 12 in 1882 when she came with her family to homestead a ranch in Yavapai County, virtually unschooled and with only the gloomiest of prospects for making a name for herself. She attended a log school four miles from the ranch for a year and then boarded in nearby Prescott for another year of schooling. That was the end of her formal education, but she devoted the rest of her life to learning – from books and journals, and from the hundreds of pioneer Arizonans she interviewed and wrote about.

She never married, but was wed to preserving oral history and collecting artifacts which eventually found a home in the fascinating Prescott museum that bears her name. Sharlot's interests were many: gaining statehood for Arizona – writing both prose and poetry of unusual quality – taking leading roles in both state and national politics – and especially preserving the log "Governor's Mansion" that housed the first Arizona territorial government in 1864. It was to that building that she agreed in 1927 to move her extensive collection. In 1909 she was appointed the first Territorial Historian, and thus became the first woman to hold a government office in Arizona.

Among her lasting achievements was that of bringing the remains of famed mountain man Paulino Weaver, Prescott's first citizen, from California to her museum grounds for reburial. Unfortunately, George W. P. Hunt, the first governor of the new state, did not appreciate her great talents and her national reputation. Hunt terminated her and abolished the office she held with such pride.

After Sharlot's death in 1943, a host of her admirers carried on the work she had begun, and today the Sharlot Hall Museum is one of the most prestigious of its kind in the Southwest. Historical researchers find it a gold mine of information, and the many thousands of visitors who flock to its exhibits each year see first-hand how pioneers lived and worked here 150 years ago. It was no surprise that Sharlot Hall was one of the first to be elected to the new Arizona Women's Hall of Fame in 1981.

This and That

Like a quilt stitched by a pioneer housewife, this final section is a conglomeration of colorful tidbits – bits of scraps and tatters drawn from more than two centuries of Arizona living: a snippet of comedy here, a tale of tragedy there, and some little known information mixed in.

Who were those crazy German boatmen? How did an unlettered boy with a talent for cartooning grow up to win a Pulitzer Prize? How did the Heard Museum come to be? Why did a secretive old Jerome priest hoard a small fortune?

If you find the answers to those questions you might go on to read about the sure-fire home remedies relied on by isolated 19th century ranchers. Or how Oklahoma mysteriously found its way to southern Arizona. Or the simple invention that made a huge contribution to Arizona growth.

Somewhere in this jumble of unrelated trivia you may find a story that you'll remember for years to come.

I hope so.

When Oklahoma Came to Arizona

When the musical "Oklahoma!" became such a hit on Broadway in the early 1950s it was decided to produce a movie version of the classic show. Director Fred Zinnemann scoured the Oklahoma countryside looking for a suitable site for filming, but there were too many oil wells, automobiles, airplanes and people in the way. Somebody suggested that the San Rafael Valley, north of Nogales in far southern Arizona, would have the untouched rural scenery he wanted. One look at the grass-carpeted hills studded with groves of live oak in the area was enough to convince him.

An all-star cast was assembled and shooting began in the summer of 1954. Gordon MacRae (Curly), Shirley Jones (Laurie), Rod Steiger (Judd Fry), Eddie Albert (Ali Hakim), James Whitmore (Andrew Carnes), Gloria Grahame (Ado Annie) and the rest of the company checked in at a Nogales hotel.

Zinnemann encountered early problems: The corn that was supposed to be "as high as an elephant's eye" was slow in maturing, so gardeners force-fed it with a variety of fertilizers. When it was deemed high enough, someone calculated that each ear had cost more than four dollars. For a love scene in the peach orchard, they brought in hundreds of wax peaches and tied them to the branches of trees in a grove. The hot afternoon sun started to melt the ersatz peaches, however, so workers had to bring them in after each day's shooting and reattach them the next day.

There was no house nearby that looked like Aunt Eller's, so they built the shell of one on the site and shot the interior scenes in Hollywood. Because Will Parker, played by Gene Nelson, was supposed to arrive from Kansas City on the train, Zinnemann found a picturesque 60-year old depot not far away and simply hung a sign reading "Claremore" over the one reading "Patagonia." There was no way to hide the un-Oklahoma-like mountains on the horizon, so the director simply hoped nobody would notice. But you can look for them in several scenes next time you see the movie.

Now the transformation was complete. The cast and company drove up from Nogales each morning and returned each evening until all the shots were safely in the can. Too soon, the company departed, leaving the lush range to the cattle and cowboys.

But the memories of the summer when a part of Arizona became Oklahoma! live on.

The Man Who Put Arizona on the World Map

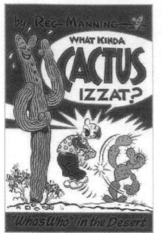

No one ever profited more from a high school class than young Reg Manning. The timid freshman from Kansas City enrolled in Cordelia Perkins' Phoenix Union High art class in 1919, and when the school term ended he had found a lifetime profession, met his future bride, and gained a love of Arizona that grew ever stronger throughout his next 67 years of life. Who could have guessed that this sickly, fatherless, dirt-poor youngster was destined to be an internationally famous editorial cartoonist and one of his era's most successful publicists of Arizona's wonders.

Reg could not afford to go to college, but labored through a series of dead-end jobs until 1926, when he was hired by the *Arizona Republican* (now *Republic*) on a trial basis as a photographer and, incidentally, as a cartoonist. Soon he was drawing an occasional editorial cartoon and before the year was out he was creating a full-page Sunday cartoon extravaganza full of humor and wisdom, which he called "The Big Parade." That feature ran for 22 years and was the first thing most Arizonans turned to on Sunday mornings. Reg published a dozen popular books about Arizona over the years, several of which are still on sale in bookstores and curio shops. Those books, including the best-selling "What Is Arizona Really Like?" and "What Kind of Cactus Izzat?" brought him worldwide fame and lured untold thousands to his adopted state.

But it was his editorial cartoons, syndicated across America and in many other countries, that earned him the most secure niche among the great Arizonans of all time.

He chronicled the Depression, World War II, Korea, Viet Nam, and the space age, winning praise and damnation from those in power around the globe. Harry Truman and Ike Eisenhower asked for his cartoons, but Lyndon Johnson – with 70 requests – asked for and received the most. He also took pride in taking under his wing a Phoenix Union High student named Bill Mauldin, who won undying fame during World War II as "the G.I.'s cartoonist."

Manning's crowning achievement, the Pulitzer Prize for editorial cartooning, came in 1951. He called it simply "Hats" and in it he decried the delays of top-hatted diplomats in prolonging the Korean War while American boys were dying with holes in their helmets.

The Dam That Made Metro Phoenix Possible

Teddy Roosevelt predicted it, speaking at the Tempe Normal School on March 19, 1911: "Because of this (Roosevelt) dam, you will see the day when 75,000 – maybe even 100,000 – people will live in this valley!"

Teddy had just returned from dedicating the gigantic dam which bears his name. It made possible today's Salt River Project, which provides water and power for nearly three million people, and created Roosevelt Lake, the world's largest man-made body of water at that time. For more than six years, horse-drawn wagons had been making the perilous journey up to the dam site over the precipitous Apache Trail, carrying untold tons of construction materials. At the site, hundreds of men hewed gigantic blocks of stone from the hillsides and made cement from the native limestone and clay.

When it was finished, the dam stood 280 feet high and 723 feet long. The waters of the Salt River behind it created a lake with a shoreline of 128 miles. It was in 1959 that Congress, at the urging of Senator Barry Goldwater, adopted its present official name: Theodore Roosevelt Dam. Barry, it seems, was concerned that people might think the dam was named for that other President Roosevelt.

In 1996 the dam was raised to 357 feet, increasing the lake capacity by 20 percent to serve the needs of central Arizona's skyrocketing population. How vital to the lives of all Arizonans is this dam and lake, and how vulnerable they are to terrorists, was illustrated in 1998 by the success of a 12-year-old computer hacker who broke into the operational systems and for a time had complete control of the floodgates.

Those "Lungers" – the Untouchables

Tuberculosis victims were like the lepers of ancient times: unclean, unfit to live in normal society, forced to exist or die in desert colonies. TB was the curse of the late 19th and early 20th centuries, and its unfortunate victims clustered by the thousands near Phoenix, Tucson, Prescott, and other communities. Doctors from all over the nation sent their TB (also called consumption) patients to Arizona in the hope that they would recover in our clean air and baking sunshine.

Phoenix had its Sunnyslope, where many hundreds fought for their lives in tents or shacks. In Tucson, Tentville housed those too poor to be treated in specialized hospital facilities. Some lungers sought relief in the Arizona high country. Prescott at the end of the 19th century had seven large TB sanitoriums, the best known of which was Dr. John Flinn's "Pamsetgaaf," named by Dr. Flinn from the capital letters of his prescription for TB recovery: "Pure Air, Maximum Sunshine, Equitable Temperature, Good Accommodations and Food." His patients lived in the bright sunshine, ate a rigidly prescribed diet, and slept outdoors in the coldest weather.

Even the darkest clouds often have silver linings: The decades-long TB scourge brought Arizona some of its most illustrious citizens. Among them were six future governors, Senator Paul Fannin's family, ASU president Grady Gammage, Barry Goldwater's mother, and Walter Winchell. Oh, yes, and gunslinger Doc Holliday, too.

Dr. Flinn's son Robert later founded the Flinn Foundation, Arizona's largest health-oriented charity. There was a sad P.S. to the story of TB in Arizona. Just as it was waning in 1918 the influenza epidemic killed many hundreds in the state. So devastating was that dread disease that for a time both Phoenix and Tucson residents had to wear masks whenever they ventured into contact with others.

The Heards: They Left Their Mark

Young Dwight B. Heard knew how to succeed in business without really trying: He married the boss's daughter. Launching his career with the Chicago wholesale hardware giant Hibbard-Spencer-Bartlett Co. (now True Value) in 1886, he caught the eye of wealthy Adolphus Bartlett who made Dwight his protégé and in 1893 gave his daughter, Maie, to him in marriage.

Two years later Dwight suffered a near-fatal lung disease and came to Phoenix to regain his health. Within a few months he was busy transforming the sleepy desert village into a vibrant young city. Cattle and real estate were his tools. His Bartlett-Heard Land and Cattle Company near South Mountain became much of south Phoenix, and his Los Olivos subdivision at Central Avenue north of McDowell soon became the most prestigious in the city.

In 1912 Dwight became enchanted with Teddy Roosevelt's Bull Moose Party and bought *The Arizona Republican* newspaper to promote his candidate. Not long thereafter he built the imposing Heard Building in downtown Phoenix to house it. Later publishers changed the paper's name to *The Arizona Republic*.

Both Dwight and his wife Maie were among the most generous philanthropists in Arizona. She was responsible for developing one of the best-known attractions in Phoenix: the Heard Museum. The Heards first collected primitive art from around the world, but their home soon bulged with items from their travels. So Maie decided to specialize in Native American art and lore, and opened the Heard Museum at 2301 North Central Avenue in 1929. Sadly, Dwight died a few months before the museum opened. Maie continued enlarging the Heard's collections until she died in 1951 at age 83, on the 22nd anniversary of her husband's death.

How Air Conditioning Changed Our History

Arizona's state motto is "Ditat Deus" (God Enriches), but one day it may be supplanted by a new one: "But It's a DRY Heat." That's our usual answer to the question so often asked by outsiders: "How do you stand your blistering summers?"

But the more accurate response is "Air conditioning." We can thank those wonderful cooling machines for transforming our little frontier backwater, one-Congressman state into a national power and making Phoenix the sixth largest city in America in little more than six decades.

It was about 1932 when young Gust Goettl started experimenting with ways to cool his niece's bedroom. He and his brothers, Adam and Bill, ran a small sheet metal shop in Phoenix. Gust put together a box with a fan inside to suck air through pads of wet excelsior and evaporation cooled the air, which was funneled through metal ducts to the interior of a house. The contraption worked so well that the Goettls were soon putting it into mass production, and Arizona summers suddenly became bearable, thanks to what we now call "swamp coolers."

More sophisticated, and much more expensive, air conditioners were being installed at that time in a few Phoenix hotels, theaters, and department stores, but evaporative coolers were used in most homes for several decades. Before the 1940s, most families sweated out the days, and tried to survive on summer nights by sleeping outdoors under wet sheets (while fighting off hungry mosquitoes) or taking refuge on screened porches. But once affordable cooling became available, newcomers from the Midwest and much of the rest of the country flocked to Arizona. That didn't please everybody. One long-time Arizonan, a hard-bitten Democrat, complained bitterly. "We didn't have all those damned Republicans here before we had air conditioning!" he moaned.

Why Zane Grey Left Arizona

Zane Grey trained as a dentist in his home town of Zanesville, Ohio, but he soon found that he hated that occupation and headed west to make his fortune as a writer. He succeeded magnificently, and his thirty novels with western themes did more to entice newcomers than all the millions of tax dollars spent on promoting tourism.

Arizona was his special love. From the day in 1906 when he was married at the Grand Canyon he explored this raw territory, hunted and fished its forests and streams, and wrote stories based on its colorful characters. He built four homes in Arizona, the best known of which was destroyed (and later rebuilt) in a forest fire east of Payson.

Grey was not immediately successful as a writer. His first novel was rejected by Harper's with a note from the editor that "I do not see anything in this manuscript to convince me that you can write either narrative or fiction." But his second novel, *Riders of the Purple Sage,* was accepted and became one of the best sellers of all time.

Many of Grey's novels were made into movies, and he enjoyed bringing his Hollywood friends to Arizona to hunt. In 1930 he arranged a bear hunt for them, but the Game and Fish Commission refused him a permit, saying bears were out of season. Grey was so angry at this bureaucratic put-down that he vowed never to return to Arizona again. And he never did.

Breaking the Color Barrier

Emerson Harvey was an all-around athlete at his Sacramento, California high school — a shot putter and discus thrower, a boxer, and especially a football star who played both defensive end and offensive back. But he could not compete at most colleges, and especially not in the Border Conference, made up of Texas, New Mexico, and Arizona schools. That's because Emerson Harvey was Black.

Tom Lillico, recently hired as a recruiter at Arizona State Teachers College (now ASU), threw caution to the wind in 1937 — ten years before Jackie Robinson broke the color line in baseball—and brought Harvey to Tempe. It was a risky thing to do, considering that the college had never had a Black athlete and would not let Blacks live in its dormitories or eat at its dining hall.

Coach Rudy Lavik's reservations about the new recruit melted at the first practice of the year, when Harvey showed he was one of the best players on the field. He suffered insults from his own teammates, and in his first game against a Texas squad he was bloodied and beaten by opposing linemen. "Nigger! Nigger! Nigger!" they chanted. Later a Texas Mines tackle admitted that he had attacked him with insults, knees, and fists. "I remember that he said to me, 'When are you white boys going to stop beating up on this poor nigger boy?' That got to me, and I could hardly bring myself to block him after that."

Harvey took all the punishment without complaint and now is hailed as a hero in the annals of ASU athletics. He breezed through his studies with a near "A" average and became a much-admired teacher and coach in Phoenix elementary schools. "What I did was no big thing," he said not long before his death. ASU knows better.

Who Needs a Doctor?

You're an Arizona Territory pioneer, circa 1870, on a ranch fifty miles from the nearest doctor (who doubles as a dentist and veterinarian), and your wife is enduring an excruciating struggle to deliver your tenth child. What to do? You race to the faded journal containing her mother's home remedies for almost every ailment. It says: "For difficult labor: Brew tea by dropping a wedding ring in boiling water." You follow directions and she soon delivers a healthy baby. No wonder our forefathers believed in such quaint home remedies.

Here are a few more, extracted from pioneer writings: For leg cramps: "Turn shoes upside down and slide them under the bed." For malaria (which was a common and often fatal disease in early Arizona): "Gather spider webs, roll them in the shape of a pill, and swallow twice a day." For toothache: "Take half a sheet of brown paper, roll it up and insert in the tooth, set fire to it and hold it as long as you can." Out on the range, where minor ailments were common, such remedies were often used. For rope burns, one journal advised "Rub cowboy urine on the burned area." And for hemorrhoids: "Burn tobacco and mix the ashes with lard." Where one should apply it was left unsaid.

Should a cowhand become habitually drunk, this was a sure-fire cure: "Mix sulphate of iron, magnesia, peppermint water, and nutmeg. Swallow morning and evening." If that didn't sober him up, nothing would. If he became weak and anemic this remedy was advised: "Push iron nails into an apple, leave overnight, and eat it in the morning."

Snake bite was a constant peril on the range and there were innumerable remedies advised. But this one tops them all: "Rub gunpowder and turpentine into the wound and set it on fire. If the victim does not improve, repeat the treatment." Sounds like a winner.

The Man Who Loved Mars

Percival Lowell had it all: wealth, a distinguished Boston family heritage, international fame as a mathematician, expert on Far East culture, author of several acclaimed books – the list goes on. But when he became enthralled with astronomy in 1893, he pushed everything else out of his life. He and an assistant scoured the southwestern United States searching for the ideal observatory site, one with clear night skies, easy access, and the absence of city lights. They found it on a pine-clad hill overlooking Flagstaff, Arizona Territory, at that time a village of 800 residents.

Because of Lowell's passion for the study of Mars, it soon became known as Mars Hill. Using his own funds, he acquired the land and a 24-inch telescope, built quarters for his wife and several astronomers, and in 1894 launched scientific investigations of all the planets in the solar system. So dedicated to his work was Lowell that he rarely left Mars Hill during the remaining 22 years of his life. He is buried in an imposing tomb near his original telescope.

Lowell won acclaim for identifying the orbit of an unknown dwarf planet he called "Planet X", which was discovered at Lowell Observatory after his death and named "Pluto." But he is perhaps best known for his ground-breaking studies of Mars. Years of photographing the "red planet" convinced him that there were canals on the Martian surface. These canals, he reasoned, must have been dug by intelligent beings in an effort to bring scarce water down from the polar ice cap. It was long after his death in 1916 that more powerful telescopes disproved his theory.

Today his original telescope is used only for educational purposes, serving the 70,000 visitors who flock to Mars Hill each year. There are now nine gigantic "eyes in the sky" at a half dozen Lowell Observatory sites, and the most powerful (4.2 meters) of all is being constructed at Happy Jack, Arizona, north of Payson. A staff of seventy, including noted astronomers and support specialists, conducts ongoing research, with an annual budget of more than five million dollars. Percival Lowell would be astounded if he could come back to his hill and see what his creation has become.

Never a Dull Moment in Jerome

Picturesque Jerome, perched precariously on Cleopatra Hill in Yavapai County, is a quiet town surviving as an artists' haven and retirement community today. But this rip-roaring "Billion Dollar Mining Camp" had plenty of action in the days before its fabulous copper mines played out. Gun battles once enlivened its narrow, twisting streets. Whiskey flowed freely, fortunes were won and lost at its gambling tables, and prostitution was one of its leading industries. Fires, such as the 1897 conflagration that all but wiped out the town, were commonplace. That one was started when an irate prostitute hurled a kerosene lamp at a customer and ignited a curtain.

Of particular interest was the incident involving a Catholic priest, revered as Father John, who came to Jerome in 1927. Many years later, when he was old and feeble, he spent most of each day sitting outside his church, sunning himself and his pet dogs. Then came the day when he disappeared, causing worried parishioners to break down the locked door to his private room to attend to him. They found the old priest wedged between his bed and a wall, weak and dazed. Once rescued, he refused to leave and had to be forcibly strapped to a chair and carried to the hospital, where he died soon afterward.

It was soon evident why he did not want to leave: They found silver coins stashed in dozens of cardboard boxes, milk cartons and bottles. Six thousand dollars was found in a cut-out book. In all, it was revealed that Father John had been accumulating these riches – about $70,000 worth – over many decades. His church mysteriously burned on the day he died, so the bishop decided to use the treasure to restore the sanctuary.

Where Did That Name Come From?

The year was 1876 and the date was July 4 – America's 100th birthday. A group of would-be settlers from Boston found themselves in the vast forest of northern Arizona Territory that day and decided to celebrate by stripping the branches off a pine tree and attaching a home-made American flag at its top. A small community was started near "the flag staff" and it grew faster when the Atlantic and Pacific Railway arrived in 1881. Flagstaff became the county seat of Coconino County in 1891.

Show Low, the gateway city to the White Mountain resorts, has an even more intriguing history. When Corydon Cooley and Marion Clark, co-owners of a ranch on the present site of the city, decided to split up, they played a card game called Seven-Up to determine who would keep the ranch. Cooley came within one point of winning, so Clark declared "Show low and you take the ranch." Tradition says Cooley turned up the deuce of clubs (Show Low's main street is named for it) and was declared the winner.

The town of Why at the junction of the Tucson-Ajo road with the Organ Pipe Cactus National Monument road is so named because travelers kept asking Peggy Kater why she lived there, so far from civilization. She often answered, "why not?" Tuba City in Coconino County is not named for the big bass horn, but for a Hopi chief whose name was unpronounceable by Mormon pioneers. "Tuba" was the closest they could come.

Arizonans did some strange things when they named towns. Marshall Trimble, Arizona's State Historian, likes to point out that Gila Bend is not in Gila County, but in Maricopa County; the ghost town of Pinal is in Gila County, not Pinal; Pima is in Graham, not Pima; Fort Apache is in Navajo, not Apache; and the town of Navajo is in Apache County.

Bimson 2, Depression 0

On January 1, 1933, Arizona was virtually broke. Banks were failing, people were losing their jobs and their homes, the state treasury was empty, and panic reigned. That was the day 40-year old Walter Bimson rode into Phoenix from Chicago like a knight on a white horse to take over the presidency of the Valley Bank and battle the fearsome Depression. In rapid order he hit that monster with two body blows that set spirits soaring and put Arizona on the road to recovery.

Blow No. 1 was a psychological masterpiece. He moved his desk to a spot just inside the front door to announce that he was open to new ideas. At the same time, he assembled loan officers from the bank's branches around the state and declared "Make loans! Wipe the dead loans from the books and go after new borrowers and depositors. People need money for a thousand purposes. We'll give it to them and you'll see the economy blossom!" Veteran bankers thought this brash youngster was crazy, but a grateful public soon hailed Bimson as a savior. The bank's deposits and loans soared.

Blow No. 2 was a public relations gem that old timers are still talking about. When the state ran out of money, it issued warrants to state employees which might be paid at some future time. Most stores accepted them, but at a discount of 20 to 25 percent. Bimson took out newspaper ads proclaiming that Valley Bank would accept them *at par!* It was a magnificent gamble, and it worked. The bank eventually recovered its money and made a host of friends for life.

Young Bimson did not totally conquer the Depression in Arizona. But he did avert a meltdown of the economy and gave Arizonans much needed hope for the future.

When Baghdad Came to Tempe

President Grady Gammage had a dream – a dream about a magnificent auditorium that would attract visitors from all over the world to Tempe and put his little Arizona State College on everyone's lips. Early in 1958 he took a bold step toward realization of his dream: He dared to go to the world's most celebrated architect, Frank Lloyd Wright, and ask for his help.

Gammage's wife Kathryn recalled what Wright told his associates of Gammage's visit: "What a charming fellow; but he has no money!" How true. He had no major donors to count on, and the stingy state legislature would only laugh at the idea of appropriating several million dollars for such a project.

But Gammage would not let his dream die. He invited Wright to visit the Arizona State campus, and the great architect was intrigued with a location for the auditorium on the Mill Avenue curve. Back at Taliesen West, Wright dug out the plans for a grand performance center he had drawn up for the ruler of Iraq, in Baghdad. That structure was never built, but Wright still hoped to build it somewhere. Maybe in Tempe!

So he revised the design, on a smaller scale, and invited Gammage to take a look. The president was enthralled, and soon he had several key patrons of the performing arts joining him in a campaign to sell the imaginative design to the legislature. Many of the lawmakers were less than thrilled, however, and one called it "Wright's little joke on Arizona." But support grew steadily, and at last state and private funding made it possible to start construction in May of 1962. The building had its grand opening in 1964 with a concert by the celebrated Philadelphia Orchestra, conducted by Eugene Ormandy.

Sadly, both Gammage and Wright had died in 1959. But their busts, prominently displayed in the lobby of Gammage Auditorium, remind grateful patrons of the men who brought it into being.

Oh, Those Crazy Boatmen!

From early 1942 until the end of World War II, Arizona was an armed camp. Almost every city and town had a flight training base or army installation. Not far south of Chandler, on the Gila Indian Reservation, 13,000 Japanese-American citizens were interned in a "relocation center." German, Austrian and Italian prisoners of war – nearly 17,000 in 18 different Arizona camps – were under guard.

One of the largest POW camps was in Papago Park northwest of Tempe, and it was here that one of the strangest episodes of the war took place. During 1944, resourceful German captives dug a 178-foot tunnel 14 feet under ground, disposing of the dirt in spoonfuls outside after a night of digging down below. On the night of December 23-24, 1944, twenty-five of them escaped through the tunnel to short-lived freedom in the largest POW escape of the war in America.

According to historian Lloyd Clark, three of them – artillery officers Wilhelm Gunther, Wolfgang Clarus, and Friedrich Utzolino – brought with them the makings of a canvas raft. These materials had been begged from camp guards "to repair the leaky roofs of our barracks." The trio had in their possession a map of Arizona, showing the Gila River flowing westward to the Colorado. Their plan was to assemble the raft on the banks of the Gila River and float all the way to Mexico. But when they had hiked the twenty miles to the Gila, they found only a marsh and a few puddles. The "Crazy Boatmen," as they were called ever after, were dumbfounded. "Those stupid Americans," one exclaimed. "They put blue on the map when there is no water in the river!"

Not willing to surrender peacefully, they trudged westward to a spot near Gila Bend, where they were recaptured after someone saw Utzolino's freshly-washed shorts hanging on a bush to dry.

The University of Arizona's Agonizing Birth

The University of Arizona and Arizona State University were conceived on the same day in 1885, in the final hours of the infamous Thieving Thirteenth legislature, but their birthings were five years apart and as wildly different as could be imagined. The Territorial Normal School (now ASU) was delivered almost painlessly at Tempe in 1886, but the Tucson institution suffered seemingly endless birth agonies before it breathed its first breath in 1891.

Tempe welcomed its little teachers' college, whereas Tucson treated its university like an alien monster. Why? Tucson had expected its legislative team to bring back the territorial capital from Prescott – or, if that effort failed – at least the $100,000 insane asylum. Instead, it had to accept the consolation prize: the $25,000 grant for a university. So angry were residents of the Old Pueblo that they pelted Tucson Senator C.C. Stevens with over-ripe vegetables and a dead cat when he tried to explain how it all happened.

Because Arizona Territory did not have a single high school at that time, nobody could see how a university could benefit the community. Besides, the bill authorizing the U of A stipulated that Tucson would have to provide forty acres of land for it. Despite the frenzied efforts of Tucson businessman J.S. Mansfeld to find a donor, nobody else seemed even slightly interested – until a saloon keeper and two noted gamblers reluctantly turned over a piece of barren desert land east of the town. That saved the project for the moment, but within a few months the frugal 14th Legislature came within a hair of negating the university appropriation. Then came the agonizing effort to appoint the first Board of Regents for the school. Three prominent men were appointed, but two of them declined to serve. It took another harrowing year to fill out the governing board. Finally, there was the problem of selling bonds to finance construction of the first building. Again, Tucson apathy almost killed the project. But at last the money was raised, construction started, and the University opened its doors to the first class on October 1, 1891.

Miranda: He Gave Us Our Rights

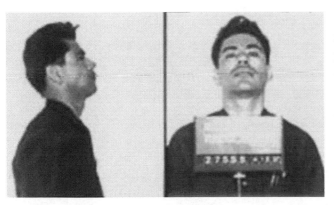

"You have the right to remain silent. You have the right . . ." It's a litany familiar to Americans everywhere, and it changed law enforcement procedures for all time to come. But few Americans – even Arizonans – are aware that it was a young Phoenix ne'er-do-well named Ernesto Miranda whose attempt to rape a young girl set the stage for the U. S. Supreme Court's historic decision on the rights of the accused.

Miranda was arrested in March, 1963, and charged with attempting to rape an 18-year old theater employee who was walking down a dark street just before midnight. At the police station he was placed in a lineup, but his victim was not completely certain that he was her attacker. However, an officer told Miranda she had identified him and, after he had confessed, had the young man write out a detailed account of the crime.

It was solely on the basis of this confession that he was convicted in a Maricopa County superior court. During the trial, the question was raised as to whether he had been advised that he did not have to testify against himself. When the arresting officer admitted that he had not given that advice, he opened a door that later was to free Miranda. Moreover, it set the stage for a series of retrials that were climaxed by the 1966 Supreme Court ruling in the young man's favor and made the "Miranda warnings" mandatory in every arrest since that time.

There was no happy ending to this story. After lengthy stays in prison for repeated crimes, Miranda was finally released in late 1975, but he was a free man for only a month. During an afternoon of drinking in a Phoenix bar he and two other men became embroiled in a brawl. Suddenly one of them pulled out a knife and stabbed Miranda to death.

Meet the Author

When he was eight years old and living in Chanute, Kansas, Dean Smith was an inveterate tree climber. One day he fell twenty feet from a slippery branch and broke both bones in both wrists. Looking with horror at those misshapen wrists, he wailed "I'll never write again!" That prediction must go down as one of the most inaccurate ever spoken, because writing has been his lifelong passion.

With ten years of newspaper reporting, more than a hundred articles in national and regional magazines, and a shelf full of books in his career, he has published more words than he cares to remember.

He has had other interests, of course – 27 years as an Arizona State University administrator – long service with the Air Force Reserve as a liaison officer for the Air Force Academy – a tormenting half century of watching his golf game go from mediocre to horrible – church and community service, and enjoying his wonderful wife and family.

He and Jean now live in the active retirement community of Friendship Village in Tempe, Arizona.

His family came to Arizona in 1933 and he graduated from Glendale High School in 1940. During World War II he served as an Army Air Corps communications officer at numerous bases, the last of which was on Adak Island in the Aleutians. He has earned bachelor's and master's degrees from what is now Arizona State University and has never stopped learning – about a myriad of subjects – in the years since college.

Perhaps his most ardent wish is to demonstrate through his writings and occasional lectures that history can be intriguing and fun.

Books by Dean Smith

Barry Goldwater: The Biography of a Conservative (with Rob Wood), Avon Books

Conservatism, Avon Books

La Gloria Escondida (bio of Pedro Guerrero), Sims Publishing

The Best of Reg (Reg Manning bio), Arizona Republic

The Sun Devils (ASU football history), ASU Alumni Assn.

The Goldwaters of Arizona, Northland Press

Brothers Five (Babbitt family history), Arizona Historical Foundation

Tall Shadows (Getz family history), Globe Corporation

The Flinn Legacy, Flinn Foundation

Arizona Pathways, Arizona Highways

The Road to Statehood, Arizona Highways

Tempe: Arizona Crossroads, Tempe Historical Society

Glendale: Century of Diversity, City of Glendale

Grady Gammage, ASU Foundation

A Tale of Two Families (Tremaines and Chilsons), Bar-T-Bar Publishing

The Meteor Crater Story (Meteor Crater Enterprises)

I Was There (with Rep. John Rhodes), Northwest Publishing, Inc.

The Fains of Lonesome Valley, Lonesome Valley Press

The Great Arizona Almanac, Westwinds Press

Arizona Goes to War (ed), University of Arizona Press

Arizona Ghost Towns and Mining Camps (ed.), Arizona Highways

Travel Arizona: The Back Roads (ed.), Arizona Highways

Bibliography

Some of the sources used in this book and recommended for further reading by those interested in the rich tapestry of Arizona history.

Wagoner, Jay J., *Arizona Territory, 1863-1912,* University of Arizona Press, Tucson, 1970

Wyllys, Rufus K., *Arizona: The History of a Frontier State,* Hobson and Herr, Phoenix., 1950

Sonnichsen, C. L., *Tucson: The Life and Times of an American City,* University of Oklahoma Press, Norman, 1982

Shadegg, Stephen, *Arizona Politics,* Arizona State University, Tempe, 1986

Trimble, Marshall, *Roadside History of Arizona,* Mountain Press Missoula, 1986

Sheridan, Thomas E., *Arizona: a History,* University of Arizona Press, Tucson, 1995

Martin, Douglas, *Yuma Crossing,* University of New Mexico Press, Albuquerque, 1954

Acknowledgments

So many people joined the author in volunteering time and talents to the production of this edition of Arizona Nuggets that it would be impossible to thank them all. In lieu of money we have been richly rewarded in the knowledge that proceeds of book sales will go to charitable endeavors.

I especially want to thank Ron Behee for his expertise and patience over several years in solving computer problems and supervising the many details of final publication.

Jennifer Hanson, who designed the cover, is also to be thanked. No one could have been a more enthusiastic partner than David Nye, president of the Friendship Village of Tempe Kiwanis Club, along with his many associates in the club.

Longtime friend and colleague Marshall Trimble wrote the Foreword and let me steal some of the results of his research.

And all these talented people, some of whom have departed this earth, made significant contributions:

Especially helpful by allowing me to interview them were: members of the Goldwater and Babbitt families; Senator Carl Hayden and Congressman John Rhodes and his wife Betty; Pulitzer winning cartoonist Reg Manning; Elliott Roosevelt; former ASU president Grady Gammage and his wife Kay; TV icon Ladmo (Ladd Kwiatkowski); former University of Arizona president Richard Harvill; and many others.

Finally, for the many historians whose publications were helpful to me in providing information and checking facts, including Rufus K.Wyllys, Thomas Sheridan, Bert Fireman; Douglas Martin, C. L. Sonnichsen, Don Dedera, Jana Bommersbach, Jay J. Wagoner, Ernest Hopkins, Sharlot Hall, Gary Stuart, Ross Rice, Byrd Granger, Earl Zarbin, and Lloyd Clark.

Illustrations in the book are from several collections, especially those of the Arizona Historical Society, the Arizona Historical Foundation, and Southwest Studies of Scottsdale Community College.

Made in the USA
San Bernardino, CA
06 February 2016